RE-TYRED

RE-TYRED

Discovering India

Sara McMurry

Matador
9 Priory Business Park,
Wistow Road, Kibworth Beauchamp,
Leicestershire, LE8 0RX
Tel: 0116 279 2299
Email: books@troubador.co.uk
Web: www.troubador.co.uk/matador
Twitter: @matadorbooks

ISBN 978 1789015 751

British Library Cataloguing in Publication Data.
A catalogue record for this book is available from the British Library.

Printed and bound by CPI Group (UK) Ltd, Croydon, CR0 4YY
Typeset in 11pt Adobe Garamond Pro by Troubador Publishing Ltd, Leicester, UK

Matador is an imprint of Troubador Publishing Ltd

FSC
www.fsc.org
MIX
Paper from responsible sources
FSC® C013604

For the children I taught in India,
and the friends I made there.

The names of children in this book have been changed.

CONTENTS

Prologue 1

Chapter 1: First Impressions 5

Chapter 2: Return to Rajasthan 22

Chapter 3: Volunteering in Shiv 36

Chapter 4: Gods and Men North and South 79

Chapter 5: Volunteering in Lalsot 90

Chapter 6: Caste and Marriage 125

Chapter 7: Learning Hindi in Jaipur 138

Chapter 8: Volunteering in Himachal Pradesh 164

Chapter 9: Volunteering in Kolkata 199

Epilogue 232

PROLOGUE

One afternoon my friend and I entered a tiny shop in the desert town of Jaisalmer in north-west India. We were lured by little carvings of elephants and camels, statuettes of Hindu gods and notebooks of handmade paper with covers of tooled camel skin or brightly coloured silk.

"What are you doing in Rajasthan?" the shopkeeper asked.

So we told him about our work as volunteers in rural schools in the region, and he told us about his family, and his brother working as a doctor in Sweden. Then he said:

"But what do you do when you are at home?"

When I explained that I was retired he said:

"Don't say 'retired' – you know tyres on wheels? You are re-tyred, and starting a new life."

* * *

I had indeed started a new life. Shortly after retiring from my university lectureship I discovered India and fell in love with it. I found warmth, light and brilliant colour, in stark contrast to the cool damp pastel shades of home. The chaos and vibrancy of life there exhilarated me. I returned again and again over the next seven years, to work as a volunteer, and to explore the huge country from the Hindi-speaking north to the Dravidian states of the south. As a volunteer I was privileged to spend time with local communities, and to see a way of life that holiday-makers miss as they flit from one tourist centre to another.

On three occasions I volunteered in rural villages. Life in the countryside seems timeless – a vision of what it would have been in Europe hundreds of years ago. There are no big advertising hoardings or supermarkets, often no mains water or drainage, and the electricity supply – when it exists – is erratic. Camels, oxen and donkeys provide transport. Crops are harvested with sickles, and rice seedlings planted out by women bent double in flooded paddies. Yet the past co-exists with the present. Many people have mobile phones, and a few have television. In slightly more prosperous areas I occasionally saw a tractor, but elsewhere people had cobbled together ramshackle (and unauthorised) vehicles from old motorbike engines attached to a chassis which might once have been a cart.

I found supermarkets in the cities of Jaipur and Kolkata, but in general they were few and far between. Far more numerous were the small local food shops, independent of any commercial chain. The best place to buy fresh vegetables and fruit was always from one of the many stalls or markets. There were a few shopping malls in the big cities that bore some resemblance to a shopping centre at home, and boasted a branch of an international store such as Marks and Spencer or United Colors of Benetton. But in Barmer, a large town with a population of over 80,000, which is the administrative capital of a district in the Thar desert, the mall I found bore little resemblance to any in Europe. It was more like a collection of market stalls transported into the interior of a two-storey concrete building.

My TEFL (Teaching English as a Foreign Language) guide suggested topics for the children to talk about. One was 'A visit to the department store', and another 'A day at the seaside'. I would have found it hard to explain to the village children what a department store was, and they lived thousands of kilometres from the sea, with not even a large lake anywhere in the vicinity. A day's holiday for them was more likely to be a religious festival, with a visit to a temple, drumming, music and dancing, and perhaps fireworks after dark. To teach in village schools I needed to change my perspective and try to understand the way the children lived. Fairy stories meant more to them than tales based on the lives of modern European children. Their games required few toys. I saw them bowling hoops made from old bicycle wheels, marking out a grid for hopscotch in the dusty street, and playing cricket whenever they had the luxury of a ball, and a stick to use as a bat.

* * *

India is so large, its population so diverse, that the inhabitants of one region do not always fully understand those of another. In Kerala I commented to my southern Indian guide that most restaurants were serving fish and many offered meat as well, whereas in Rajasthan restaurants were vegetarian unless they displayed a sign saying 'Non veg'.

"Oh, that's because there are so many high Brahmins in Rajasthan," he replied. "It is they who are vegetarians."

But most of the people I met and worked with in the north were not Brahmins, high or otherwise, yet many of them were vegetarian.

* * *

Tourists, and those who visit India's universities or businesses professionally, are immersed in prosperous modern India. Though they may see slums and people living on the street, they have little real exposure to the lives of the poor and underprivileged. Most of the big aid agencies work in urban areas, so many volunteers have no experience of rural life. I was particularly fortunate to volunteer both in villages and in a city, and I saw for myself that a life of poverty in a rural community is completely different from the life of a street or slum dweller in a city.

On every visit I was surrounded by dramatic scenery and novel experiences, and I saw new aspects of this endlessly fascinating sub-continent, its people and their customs. What I learnt was sometimes distressing, at other times inspiring, always intriguing. I did not travel to India intending to write a book about it, but back in Ireland I found people so interested in my experiences that I felt impelled to record what I had seen, and to show, like a series of snapshots, the India that I discovered.

Chapter 1

FIRST IMPRESSIONS

I had never had any desire to go to India. I was deterred by the thought of sticky heat, mosquitos, and poverty and dirt in crowded cities. The Taj Mahal was reputed to be very beautiful, but I had seen pictures of it – I did not need to go there. As a child I had been fascinated by Hillary and Tensing's conquest of Everest and would have leapt at a chance to visit the beautiful valleys and high mountains of Nepal. And I had dreamed of visiting Tibet, rimmed by the high barrier of the Himalayas, with its cold barren landscape, Buddhist monasteries perched on hillsides, and prayer flags fluttering in the wind beside lonely lakes. But I had never seriously contemplated travelling in Asia.

Then, a few months after I retired, I met a friend for lunch.

"Come to India next February," she said. "I'm organising a two-week tour. All you need to do is get a visa and some inoculations. Wear shoes not sandals because of the snakes, and bring a cardigan – it could be cool in the evenings."

It was to be a coach tour, covering two and a half thousand kilometres through north-west India, visiting the great Mughal palaces of Rajasthan, staying in luxury hotels, accompanied by an Indian guide.

"It's too good a chance to miss," Brian, my husband, said. "We would never organise a trip like this for ourselves. Let's go."

So we went, though as I read about Rajasthan in travel guides I regretted that the tour would take us to this flat and arid region rather than to the foothills of the Himalayas.

Brian and I travelled from a cold, damp Dublin to the sun and warmth of a Rajasthan winter; from women clad fashionably in black under grey clouds to women wearing brightly coloured saris under skies which were clear and blue. It was as if I had stepped out of a black and white movie into a technicolour film – like Dorothy entering the land of Oz.

* * *

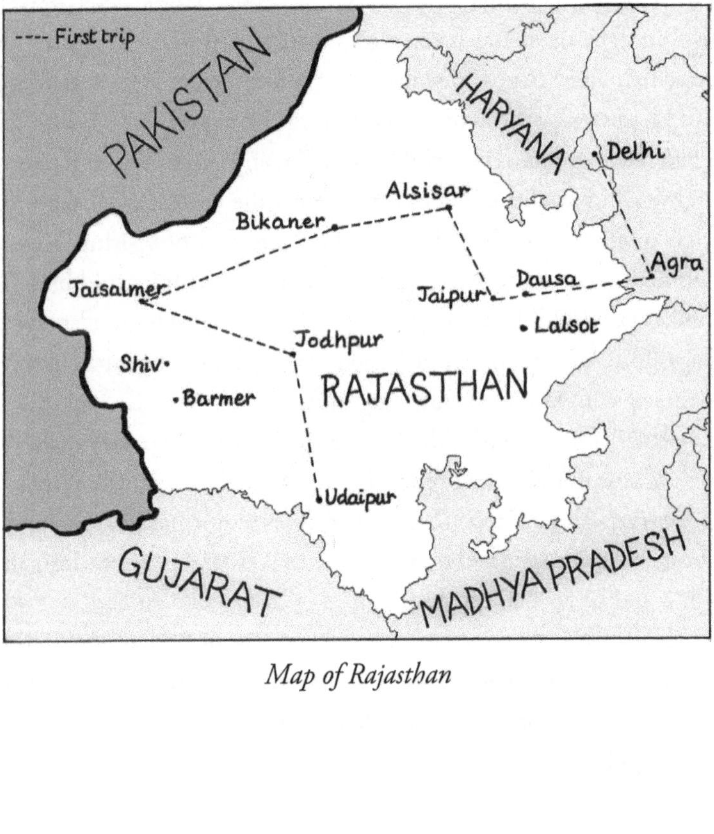

Map of Rajasthan

India began to work its magic on me from the first morning. We breakfasted in Delhi, looking out on a hotel garden bright with scarlet flowers, where green parakeets shrieked as they flew between the palm trees, and overhead black kites soared and wheeled in a cloudless sky.

Over the next two weeks I marvelled at magnificent forts of dark red sandstone and was dazzled by white marble pavilions with elegant Mughal arches and delicate floral decorations. The Taj Mahal was more beautiful in real life than in any picture or photograph. The weather was perfect – sunny and warm, but not too hot. In the strange deserted city of Fatehpur Sikri, abandoned in 1585 just fourteen years after it was completed, only the bare, leafless branches of deciduous trees reminded me that it was winter here.

I wandered round sumptuous palaces, royal museums and richly decorated *havelis* – the mansions of long gone merchants who became rich on traffic in opium and silk. We drove through the Thar desert, where forts the colour of sand perched on rocky outcrops, and finally came to the beautiful city of Udaipur on Lake Pichola, rimmed by the ancient hills of the Aravalli range.

But what fascinated me more than the museums, forts and palaces, with their long histories and exotic art and architecture, was the teeming life of India all around me, not only in the towns and cities where we stopped, but seen through the coach window as we travelled. The books, which I had brought to read during the long drives from one tourist centre to another, remained unopened.

India is a country of stark contrasts. Monumental palaces and forts rise like islands above oceans of dilapidated buildings on streets strewn with rubbish. Smartly dressed men and women in expensive cars drive past people with nowhere to live but the street. Women cook food, and children play and sleep, under bridges supporting raised sections of the Delhi metro.

Wherever we stopped, crowds of hawkers gathered round, trying to sell us postcards and trinkets. In spite of their poverty their clothes, though worn and sometimes tattered, were clean.

"Look at them," said Amitabh, our guide. "They are not sitting around waiting for help. They are finding ways to make a living, selling things and offering to clean your shoes."

Indeed I saw comparatively few beggars during the tour, and those I did see were at tourist sites. Those that really upset me were outside the Taj Mahal. There, men with withered and misshapen limbs dragged themselves around on little trolleys. They had been maimed deliberately to provide them with a living as beggars. Amitabh told us that a few years ago such beggars had become less common, but unfortunately the boom in tourism had led to a revival in their numbers.

That first morning we emerged into a maelstrom of vehicles. A *tuk-tuk* (motorised rickshaw), bursting at the seams with children in smart school uniforms, slipped rapidly into a hardly perceptible gap in front of our coach. Cars and buses overtook us on both sides. I looked down on a moped where a small boy sat between the arms of his father, who was driving, while his mother and sister rode pillion. A cyclist veered suddenly across the front of the car beside us to take a right turn, and hordes of pedestrians risked death to cross the street between the never-ending streams of traffic. But I found this chaos exciting rather than frightening. Drivers seemed to know the width of their cars and *tuk-tuks* to within millimetres, and I did not see one vehicle so much as scrape another.

We embarked in pairs on cycle rickshaws and were pedalled through narrow streets. A scraggy white horse in blinkers brought everything to a halt as it attempted to pull a laden cart out into the stream of cars, motorbikes and rickshaws. Pedestrians walked briskly down the middle of the road, overtaking the stalled traffic. The man pedalling my rickshaw was not young, and this seemed backbreaking work.

"I come from Nepal," he told me. "I have no education, so I can't get a good job there. With this work in Delhi I earn enough to send money home to my family."

"Buy my postcards?" asked a little boy of about eight years old, as I followed the others into the Red Fort.

"No," I replied, "I have to keep up with my group."

But he was not deterred.

"When you come out I will remember you, and you will remember me – look, I have a lovely white shirt."

And indeed he had. (It amazed me that the men, no matter how tattered, were able to appear in Persil-white shirts, especially when I saw the women washing clothes in filthy brown water.) When he claimed me on my way out, with a winning smile showing white teeth to match his shirt, I bought postcards from him.

In the grand surroundings of Lutyens' Delhi, a small group of shabbily dressed people, one man limping on a crutch because he had only one leg, was allowed to pass the security post. Security was tight, as it was only three months since the terrorist attack in Mumbai. We had been stopped from walking further up the road towards the President's residence and were standing admiring the Lutyens buildings which now house Indian government offices.

"I am allowing these people through," the soldier on duty explained, "because they have a petition to present to the President."

In spite of the enormous inequality in wealth and opportunity in Indian society, these poor people were allowed access to the Presidential palace.

* * *

The road from Delhi to Agra is part of what was once the Grand Trunk Road which ran from Calcutta (now Kolkata) to Kabul. The mile posts still have the holes that were provided for carrier pigeons to rest in. On this and all the big main roads there were huge lorries. They were decorated with painted slogans and pictures, draped with tinsel and flowers, and heavily overloaded. Many had a sign on the back saying 'HORN PLEASE', and our coach driver would always hoot as a signal when he was about to overtake.

Men rode in the backs of open trucks, their faces swathed in scarves against the dust, like desert nomads. Trucks, lorries, cars and buses shared the roads with more ancient forms of transport. I saw men walking, leading heavily laden donkeys, and others driving wooden carts pulled by plodding oxen. Camels, looking down their superior noses, padded along pulling low two-wheeled carts piled high with full sacks on which the driver perched.

"There are never more than three camels in a train nowadays," Amitabh told me. "Not so long ago there would have been much longer trains with maybe a dozen or more camels."

On a stretch of dual carriageway I was horrified to see a car travelling in the wrong direction. But other drivers appeared unperturbed, and I soon discovered this was standard practice. Our lunch stop was on the other side of the dual carriageway, and to reach it our driver found a gap in the concrete barrier so that he could turn back towards it. But when we left, he made for the same gap to regain our original side of the road, even though it meant travelling against the oncoming traffic.

A white car, decorated all over with tinsel and flowers, carried a newly married couple. And once I saw a young man wearing a gorgeous gold and scarlet tunic with a matching turban-like headdress and riding a white horse. The horse, too, was decked in scarlet and gold, its harness embellished by a plume of bright red feathers.

"He is going to fetch his bride to the wedding ceremony," explained Amitabh.

Small farming settlements were fenced with thorny acacia branches to keep out wild animals. Humped cows or velvet-black water buffalo were tethered outside small single-storey houses, where women sat shaping cow pats to dry for fuel. In the villages tiny stalls were piled high with mouth-watering displays of fresh fruit and vegetables. After dark, village markets were lit by the gentle yellow glow of lamps and decorated with strings of little white or green lights like Christmas decorations. People shopped and gossiped, or sat eating at open-air tables.

There were so many birds. A flash of turquoise wings marked the flight of an Indian roller, bright green bee-eaters with long tails perched on telegraph wires, and the rufous wings of coucals were bright against their sooty backs. Red-wattled lapwings stood on long yellow legs beside the road with surprised looks on their faces.

One evening, after driving for hours through a flat landscape, I thought the way ahead was blocked by sandy hills. But our road found a gap between high cliffs, and we entered the city of Jaipur. Here elephants with painted faces padded along in the traffic, and a band of men playing bugles and drums marched at the side of the street in smart white uniforms and red turbans with a long streamer down the back.

* * *

The ancient rocks of Rajasthan yield precious and semi-precious stones. Jaipur is known for its jewellers, and Jaisalmer for its silver work. In a silversmith's we were seated on low cushioned benches around a large mattress which covered the floor. One after another men brought in sacks of silver and emptied at our feet piles of bracelets, necklaces, earrings and ornate boxes. It was like a scene from the *Arabian Nights*.

In an Agra workshop I watched men sitting on the ground painstakingly shaping tiny petals, leaves and stems from slivers of semi-precious stones – blue lapis lazuli, green malachite, red and yellow cornelian, turquoise. Then they pasted them carefully into precisely shaped indentations in hard white Indian marble. The showroom above was an Aladdin's cave of delicately decorated plates and dishes, bowls and even tabletops. This craft has been passed down through the generations of families who created the beautiful inlaid marble decorations on the Taj Mahal in the seventeenth century.

"I learnt from my father, and he from his, and so on back to the days of Shah Jahan," the owner of the workshop said. "But my children are not interested. They want easier jobs. Inlaid marble is produced by machines in factories now, and my craft will soon die out."

When we visited Varanasi the following year, Brian and I heard a similar story. In a silk weavers' establishment beautiful lengths of pure silk were still being woven on hand looms, some of them the very ancient pre-Jacquard type, where the pattern is determined by a man manipulating knotted cords on one side of the loom, while a second man passes the shuttle back and forth on the other. There were only a few looms in the shop because most of the work was done by people in their homes – a cottage industry in a city. But this craft is dying too. The silk produced by this slow, painstaking work is very expensive, and cheap fabric for saris is imported from mechanised industries in China.

"Most people cannot afford to buy our handmade silk," said the weaver. "Now it is bought mainly for wedding saris, or by tourists."

But the handmade fabric, like the hand-decorated marble, is much finer and more delicately beautiful than anything made by a machine. These are art forms rather than industries.

* * *

Everywhere in public parks and hotel grounds I saw little squirrels, striped like chipmunks. Amitabh told us a legend of how the squirrel got his stripes:

"The Lord Rama's beloved wife Sita had been stolen away by a wicked demon and was being held captive on an island. The monkey people came to help Lord Rama and started placing large rocks in the water to build a causeway to the island so that he could cross over and recover his wife.

"The little squirrel (who had no stripes on his back then) wanted to help. But he was too small to carry rocks and stones, so he ran into the water to wet his fur. Then he rolled in the sand and went back into the water to wash it off where the monkeys were placing their stones. He did this time and time again, and in this way made his small contribution to the causeway.

"The Lord Rama saw him and was touched by his efforts. He thanked him, and stroked his back, leaving his fingermarks as the stripes which all squirrels in India carry to this day."

I was reminded of Rudyard Kipling's *Just So Stories*. Did this Hindu legend inspire his tales of how the elephant's child acquired a long trunk and how the leopard got his spots? I thought of Kipling again in Udaipur, for there in the courtyard outside the museum, in the precincts of the Maharana's palace, was a cage with metal bars labelled 'Cage for leopard'. In *The Jungle Book*, Bagheera the black panther tells Mowgli:

"I was born among men, and it was among men that my mother died – in the cages of the king's palace at Oodeypore."

Did Kipling see the same cage that I now saw and imagine a black panther cub growing up there until he was strong enough to break the lock and escape to the jungle?

* * *

Leaving the big highways we travelled through dry, sandy countryside, with irrigated fields providing square patches of bright green in the arid landscape. Scrubby acacias gave a little shade for the occasional flock of sheep and goats. Women in bright saris – scarlet, turquoise, lime green, yellow – walked elegantly, with perfect posture, carrying shining metal pots or huge bundles of sticks on their heads. Even in the most barren areas people would appear, walking beside the road, miles from any sign of habitation.

Sometimes I glimpsed deer, half hidden by trees. Once a gazelle, a delicate fawn coloured creature with a black stripe on its flanks and ringed horns, stood poised warily for a moment before leaping away. A jackal loped across open ground in pursuit of a herd of goats.

We stopped to watch a huge flock of demoiselle cranes that was wintering beside a lake next to a tiny village. In the spring they fly back over the Himalayas to spend the summer in Tibet. These graceful birds crowded the slopes down to the water's edge. When a dog disturbed them they rose to fly round in a great flock of beating wings before settling again. The villagers had created the pond to attract the cranes, and regularly put out grain for them.

"The villagers think the cranes are auspicious. They believe they are reincarnations of past members of the community," Amitabh explained.

The road became sand with a single track of tarmac down the centre, and cars coming towards us had to move onto the sandy verge to pass by. When we met a lorry, the coach and the lorry would head straight towards one another. Every time, I thought a crash was inevitable. But at the last possible moment lorry and coach each veered off onto the sand on their nearside and passed one another safely.

One thing that struck me was that Indian tourists far outnumbered Europeans at all the big historic sites. But not so in Alsisar. In this small town, where the sandy unpaved streets were too narrow for our coach, our luggage was piled onto a camel cart while we walked the short distance to the hotel. Here our small group appeared to be the only tourists.

Alsisar was my favourite stop of the tour. It was more a village than a town, though it lay on a spur of the ancient Silk Road, and in the past rich merchants had built magnificent *havelis* there. Now the merchants had left and their homes were abandoned and decaying. But lively frescos on the outer walls still showed pictures of camels, elephants, soldiers, birds and flowers. The interiors of some had been restored to show tourists their past glory. The internal walls were covered with decorative painting, and the alcoves were studded with little pieces of concave mirror, to reflect and augment the light of candles.

Our hotel must once have been the fort of the local lord. Drums and a fanfare of trumpets greeted us, as well as the usual marigold garlands, spots of red on our foreheads, and cool drinks. The internal rooms were built round two big, elegantly porticoed courtyards, open to the sky. We ate dinner at a long table in the inner courtyard, with the night sky overhead, and afterwards I climbed up to the flat roof to look at the stars, brilliant in a dark sky unpolluted by city lights.

I had never realised before that, closer to the equator, the moon would be tilted at a different angle from that which we are used to in Europe. Here the moon lay on its back like a bowl, rather than on its side like a letter C. (When I mentioned this later to an Indian friend who had never travelled to more northern lands, he said he had always wondered why the moon was on its side on the flags of Turkey and some Middle Eastern countries.)

All was peace and quiet, except for the cries of the wild peacocks, which perched on the walls and woke me in the morning. There was no traffic, and life proceeded at a slow and gentle pace. In the village, men worked in open-fronted shops. One sold brightly coloured sheets and hangings, at another a tailor was using an old-fashioned treadle sewing machine, and next door men crafted small pieces of silver jewellery. Shopkeepers greeted us, and children called "Hello" in English. The little girls were very shy – they gave us big smiles but then turned away quickly. An older woman, her face veiled with her scarf in Hindu fashion, passed by without looking at us, but the teenage girl with her turned back to gaze curiously.

I longed to spend some time in a village like this, away from the rush and bustle of the cities.

* * *

In the city of Bikaner, in the desert region near the border with Pakistan, the streets were lined with shops and stalls, and thronged with *tuk-tuks*, bikes and mopeds. Cows and hairy pigs wandered among the pedestrians. I saw a goat standing on its hind legs to help itself from a vegetable stall while the owner's back was turned.

But the streets were too narrow for our coach to pass through, and we took a hair-raising *tuk-tuk* ride to our hotel. Whenever it turned from one street into another the *tuk-tuk* had to cross an open drain bridged by a pair of narrow metal strips exactly the right distance apart for the rear wheels. This meant that the driver had to direct his single front wheel over one of the strips and then manoeuvre so that each back wheel was exactly aligned with a strip. The drivers were adept at this and, in spite of my fears, succeeded perfectly each time, with very little decrease in speed.

A small shop in a courtyard of the hotel was stocked with beautiful silks and brocades, some already made up into elegant *kurtas*. I was attracted by a short tunic in turquoise brocade shot with rose pink, and the shopkeeper told me I could take it away to try it on. When I assured him that I was staying in the hotel he said:

"Yes, I know, you are in the room with the mirror ceiling."

(All the rooms were decorated differently, and in ours the ceiling was covered with tiny squares of glass, like those used in the rooms of the old *havelis* we had visited in Alsisar.) I was amazed that he knew exactly who I was, though I had only just arrived. All Indians seem to have a very good memory for faces. Hotel employees always knew exactly who we were and where we were, even though we never stayed in the same place for more than two nights.

In Udaipur we had to carry ID cards to pass through the gate from the Maharana's palace grounds to our hotel. On one occasion I returned alone and started to hunt for my card, but the guard said:

"Don't worry – I recognise you. I was on duty when you went out," and allowed me through.

In Udaipur again two years later I entered a shop selling cushion covers, scarves and all kinds of handicrafts. The manager came up and greeted me, saying:

"I remember you – you were here once before, with a group."

Until that moment I had not realised that I had visited that very shop on my original tour, though it had seemed vaguely familiar.

* * *

As we left the hotel in Bikaner, a holy man, dressed all in white, was going round the rooms which surrounded the main courtyard, blessing them. Religion is very much a part of Indian life, and astrology goes hand-in-hand with religion. I read in the *Times of India* that the Indian Supreme Court had been forced to retract its pronouncement that astrology was not a science. Horoscopes determine whether prospective marriage partners are suited, and the horoscope of a baby, whose family I met, determined what his name should be.

Amitabh's brother was a mathematician and astrologer. (Astrology depends on numerology.) Amitabh suggested that Eddie (who had started his career as a mathematician) might like to play a number game with his brother, while I looked on to work out how it was done. He phoned his brother and transmitted his instructions to Eddie. Although Amitabh told us that the game involved nothing more than simple arithmetic, its conclusion was surprising, and not something I could account for rationally.

First of all Eddie was asked to choose a two-figure number. He chose 49, and after a few moments Amitabh relayed the message from his brother:

"According to your choice of number you must be very religious."

Indeed Eddie is a regular attender at Mass. Then Amitabh said:

"We are going to do a sum, starting with your number, 49, and my brother says the answer will be 247."

Eddie was asked for a second two-figure number, and the astrologer promptly gave a third and asked Eddie for a fourth. Then the astrologer said:

"Now add up those four numbers," and to my surprise, and to Eddie's, they added up to 247, the answer which Amitabh's brother had predicted.

Eddie had not been keeping track of the sum, nor did he know how many numbers he would be asked for. He had no idea why he chose 99 as the fourth number – it was, he thought, a purely random choice. Yet this number had completed the sum.

After some thought I realised that the predicted total was Eddie's first number with 99 added twice, (49 + 99 + 99 = 247). Eddie's first two numbers were 49 and 23. Then Amitabh's brother supplied 76, which is the difference between 99 and 23. This completed the first 99. Eddie finished the sum with 99, (49 + 23 + 76 + 99 = 247). The surprising thing was that, without keeping count, Eddie supplied exactly the right number to reach the predicted answer.

Clearly, by working in groups of numbers adding up to 99, the astrologer could calculate very quickly how much more was needed to reach his predicted total. This much was clearly just arithmetic. If Eddie had chosen a smaller number than 99 for the fourth number, then the astrologer could have again picked the difference between it and 99 to reach the correct total. But in that case it would have been Amitabh's brother instead of Eddie who completed the sum. The game would have been trivial, only requiring the astrologer to keep count.

Amitabh himself was impressed by the outcome of his brother's game with Eddie. When I tried it with him instead of his brother, I made sure that my final number would not complete the sum, to see what would happen. Amitabh supplied a fifth number to reach the correct sum, and there was no mystery. Could the astrologer have exerted some kind of telepathic influence on Eddie?

* * *

In this region the Thar desert was not a sand sea with billowing dunes, but a stony plain where a few scrubby bushes and small deep-rooted acacia trees grew. In places, white patches of salt shimmered on the surface. I had never seen such a huge flat and empty expanse, and the sky above was a vast inverted bowl.

After a long drive through featureless desert we stopped, and I walked across the sand towards a little pool with a single small leafless tree beside it. A kingfisher perched there, then dived in a streak of turquoise into the water, before returning to its perch with its catch. Two donkeys roamed the edge of the pool, each accompanied by a white cattle egret. The beauty and isolation of this tiny oasis gave me a great sense of peace.

In the middle of nowhere we came upon a camel fair. Camels, humped cattle and water buffalo were resting under the shade of small trees and feeding from sacks of grain. Some camels stood harnessed to wooden carts, while men worked around them. Other men sat in little groups, talking after the day's bargaining was over.

In the desert near Jodhpur we visited Bishnoi craftsmen, who live in harmony with nature. They are strict vegetarians and believe in preserving all life. Some were potters, making the beautiful spherical clay pots which I saw stacked high on market stalls. When half dried the clay becomes elastic and can be beaten out so that the finished pots are amazingly thin-walled and perfectly shaped. But everywhere I went in Rajasthan I saw women carrying water in modern metal pots. The potter's craft, like that of the marble decorators and silk weavers, is dying out.

In another house, mats (called *duris*) were woven from cotton and jute. They were attractively decorated with traditional geometric designs and coloured with vegetable dyes. The Bishnoi have no mains electricity or water supply. However, they do have mobile phones, and great ingenuity. I was able to buy a *duri* using my credit card. The man of the house had a credit card machine which he attached to an ancient car battery and to his mobile phone. The contraption successfully accepted my card at the third attempt. The *duri* was packed up and posted to my son in Ireland, and when I returned home I received a delightful email from the man who sold it to me, asking me to confirm that it had arrived safely and wishing my son much pleasure in using it.

Travelling on into the south-west, flat desert gave way to the sandy Aravalli hills. A big troupe of langur monkeys, with black faces and pale silky fur, surveyed us from the bushes. Young ones leapt and played in the branches, and tiny babies clung, upside down, to their mothers' chests.

Pink bougainvillea made a splash of brilliant colour as I looked out on Lake Pichola from our hotel in Udaipur. In the middle of the lake, the shining white Lake Palace hotel glittered on its island. Early in the morning I saw men fishing from little boats with nets that looked like umbrellas made of mesh.

On our last evening, the surface of the lake reflected the orange glow left in the sky by the sunset, and ripples from the wash of a small boat cut dark lines across it. I looked up at a thin crescent moon, lying on its back like a saucer, with the planet Venus above it.

* * *

It had been a whirlwind tour, leaving me with a confusion of images and impressions. Although I had longed for mountains I found that I loved the desert, with its great flat expanses interrupted by the occasional rocky outcrop, and the pearly glow in the evening as the sun sank to the horizon.

Fourteen days seemed to me far too short a time to spend in this country. Of course, the cities were huge and crowded. I had seen enormous wealth beside great poverty, and beauty beside squalor. But some of my most vivid memories are of the genuine friendliness I met from all sorts of people. A middle-aged couple, tourists like myself at the Taj Mahal, stopped to shake hands, welcome me to their country and enquire where I came from and where I was going. A security guard beside Lake Pichola smiled at me and commented on the beautiful sunset. A little girl in school uniform smiled shyly and laid her hand on mine for a brief moment when my *tuk-tuk* was stopped in traffic.

Though so much was unfamiliar I did not find it alien. I was aware of cultural difference, but had no sense of culture shock. My overall impression was of enormous vitality and teeming life. I longed to discover more of the country and its people. On that short tour I had fallen under the spell of India, and I knew I must return.

Chapter 2

RETURN TO RAJASTHAN

Back in Ireland I dreamed of returning to India. As a tourist I had rushed from place to place, merely skimming the surface of the country. But I remembered villages seen from the coach window, where goats, chickens and hairy pigs roamed freely, cows and water buffalo chewed the cud in the shade, and women in brightly coloured saris fetched water from the well. Was there any way that I could spend time in the countryside and live for a while in a village, learning something of the people's lives?

Then, by chance, I met an old friend who had just returned from India. She had worked there for a few months as a volunteer. So I searched for Irish volunteer organisations and found one[1] offering volunteer placements in India for people over thirty, teaching English and Mathematics in rural primary schools. This sounded just what I was looking for. There were opportunities in Rajasthan or in the foothills of the Himalayas. Though I was

---

1 *The Irish Volunteer Sending Organisation*, the branch of *EIL Intercultural Learning* which sends volunteers to a variety of countries. EIL, http://www.eilireland.org, is based in Cork.

tempted by the mountains, it would be cold there during the winter, when I planned to go. So I chose to revisit Rajasthan, where the volunteer organisation had a base in the village of Shiv.

Preparations for the trip kept me busy. I was interviewed to assess my suitability as a volunteer, and had my background vetted by the police because I would be working with children. I booked my flights, applied for a visa and collected things I thought would be useful: a jar of Marmite (because my friend had returned from three months on a vegetarian diet in India with vitamin B12 deficiency), a good torch, and a copy of Rudyard Kipling's *Kim*. During my seven weeks at Shiv I re-read *Kim* with delight. Though it was written over a century before, Kipling's vivid portrayal of Indian life echoed something of what I was experiencing.

Books take space and are heavy, so, apart from *Kim*, I took only a couple of small picture books for the schoolchildren, and a paperback copy of *Teach yourself Hindi*. A friend gave me an inflatable globe, and I found an attractive set of flash cards for teaching English.

In Dublin the winter was very cold, and snow lay on the ground for the first time for over twenty years. The mains water pipes in our area were frozen, and we fetched buckets of water from a water tanker provided by the council – a foretaste of living in an area where water is scarce. As the time of departure approached people asked me:

"Haven't you got cold feet? Aren't you a little scared to be going off all by yourself?"

There were times when I wondered whether what I was doing was completely mad. But my husband and children were supportive and friends encouraged me. Though I was flying out alone, I was to be met at the airport in Delhi by someone from the Indian volunteer organisation, and I would be joining other volunteers. We were to live in a volunteer camp, in the village of Shiv in the Thar desert, and work with local children. So I encouraged myself with thoughts of warmth and colour and the fascination of India, and one cold January evening I boarded the Jet Airways flight from Heathrow to Delhi.

* * *

This second visit to India was a complete contrast to the protected, pampered luxury of my first trip, and I quickly discovered a little of the uncertainty and chaos of Indian life. I arrived in a cool and foggy Delhi expecting to find someone from the volunteer organisation waiting for me. But it was the week before the national Constitution Day holiday, and the airport arrivals hall had been cleared of all 'meeters and greeters' as a security precaution. Hordes of men were crowded outside the two exit doors on opposite sides of the hall, holding placards with names of arriving passengers, tour groups or hotels. But in neither place could I see a sign with my name on it. (When I finally met Ashvini he showed me a small piece of paper with my name scrawled across it in pencil, and I understood why I had been unable to see it.)

I had a telephone number to ring in an emergency. All I needed were some rupees and I would be able to use the public telephone next to the Aertel desk in the arrivals hall… but of course the ATM was not working. However, the Aertel staff took me under their wing. One of them phoned my emergency number twice, once to explain my predicament and again, five minutes later, to be given the mobile phone number of Ashvini, who was meeting me. Then he phoned Ashvini and told him to come and stand outside the window where I could see him.

Though I was not expecting luxury, the hotel to which Ashvini took me looked run-down. It was one of several in an area frequented by Western backpackers and tourists on a tight budget, set in a maze of dusty narrow streets festooned with electricity wires and lined with grey buildings in various states of disrepair. One that had been demolished was being rebuilt, and men with hods of bricks on their heads were climbing up bamboo scaffolding held together with rope.

My room in the hotel was small and shabby. All through the night pigeons landed with a clang on the metal air-conditioning unit outside the window, to be greeted with loud cooing by those already perched there. At four o'clock in the morning I was woken by a thunderous knocking on my door. Being all alone in a strange place I was reluctant to open the door, but then the phone rang and the hotel receptionist asked:

"Why will you not open the door to your room mate? She says you may be frightened. Are you frightened?"

I protested that I did not have a room mate, but they told me that all volunteers had room mates. So I opened the door, and Caroline, who had just arrived from the airport, fell in, apologising profusely.

Bengt, a Norwegian volunteer, had a similar experience. He was woken in the middle of the night, and to his horror a strange man was thrust into his room to share his double bed. Why had nobody explained to either of us that we would be joined by another volunteer in the middle of the night?

But the hotel staff were helpful too. One of them led me to an ATM, through dusty little streets crowded with pedestrians, bicycles, *tuk-tuks* and the occasional car (which took up nearly the whole width of the road). All the streets looked the same to me, and I would never have been able to find the way there – or back again – by myself.

The following morning, when the rest of the volunteer group had assembled, the same man took several of us on an abortive trip to get Indian sim cards for our mobile phones. On a busy narrow street the Vodafone shop was one shabby windowless building surrounded by others. But to go in was like walking through a magic portal. Inside it was spacious, clean and bright, just like a Vodafone shop back home. However, buying a sim card was fraught with difficulties. As she took away our passports to photocopy them, the assistant asked for passport-size photos as well. So our friend took us to a tiny dark shop nearby, where a young man photographed us with a hand-held camera. Only when we were on the point of paying for our sim cards were we told that we must supply a Delhi address at which we would be staying for at least three days. As we were to leave for Agra that afternoon we had to go away empty handed. Our friend seemed to feel personally responsible and apologised profusely all the way back to the hotel.

By now the whole group had arrived. My room mate Caroline was from Hungary, Tina and Lena from Sweden, Karin and Gabrielle from Germany, Bengt from Norway and Alex from the US. His daughter Joya was the only one of us under thirty. My fears of being much the oldest proved groundless. Four of us were grandparents, and three others had children and husbands at home. During the next week, as we endured late trains, lack of sleep and an intensive round of instruction and introduction to Indian life in Jaipur, their companionship kept me cheerful and full of a sense of adventure.

Ashvini was a young Rajasthani in his twenties, who was on the staff at the camp in Shiv. He was surprised and a little dismayed by our less than enthusiastic response when he asked how we liked the hotel. I felt sorry for him whenever he had to hire taxis or *tuk-tuks*, since the drivers always shouted at him and tried to extract a larger fare. As he was a gentle quiet lad he found it hard to stand up to them.

Setting off for Agra, I had my first experience of an Indian railway station. The platforms were thronged with people, many sitting or squatting on the ground in family groups, surrounded by their possessions in shabby suitcases, baskets or packs. Some were chatting, some eating and drinking, others just sat gazing into space, or slept, wrapped in shawls. Children ran here and there among the crowds, smiling shyly and eager to be photographed when they saw our cameras. Several shabbily dressed beggar children wandered round with hands outstretched, but did not pester us or the Indians they approached. Pigeons searched the platform for crumbs. The few benches were occupied by businessmen with smart briefcases and laptops, or elegantly dressed women. Dusty trains pulled by huge diesel engines thundered into the station and pulled out again packed with people, some still hanging on precariously at open doors.

We had arrived in mid afternoon, an hour before our train was due, and Ashvini discovered that it was to be five hours late. When one of us asked, slightly sarcastically:

"So, what do we do? Stand here for five hours?" he replied quite seriously :

"Well, you could sit down."

We had not yet understood that waiting patiently, sometimes for hours, was an inescapable part of Indian life.

Eventually Ashvini phoned headquarters and was told to take us by bus instead. So, after a long wait while he cancelled the train tickets, we dragged our luggage back up over the footbridge and across a very rough piece of ground to the bus terminus.

We huddled together on metal benches to wait again, cold and tired. Scruffy blue buses rattled in and departed bursting with passengers. The area around the terminus was bleak and run-down. Beyond a stretch of wasteland towered dismal grey blocks of flats. The light was beginning to fade, and the air was misty with pollution. Suddenly I heard the strident call of a bird and saw a big kingfisher perched on wires just outside the bus station. The dreary scene was magically transformed – here was a bird I would only have expected to see beside a peaceful river or lake, but it appeared perfectly at home in the heart of Delhi.

As we sat on the bus waiting for it to depart, two tall good-looking women in scarlet saris got on. Here was another anachronism. Their behaviour was in striking contrast to the quiet modesty of most Indian women in public places. They flounced down the aisle with provocative smiles and banter which was clearly bawdy, although I could not understand what they said. Though they were begging they did not plead or ask for pity. Instead they seemed completely in control of the situation and amused at the embarrassment of the men on the bus. Passengers looked away, but several gave them money. They had no intention of travelling, and got off the bus before it left.

It was not until two weeks later that an Indian colleague explained to me:

"Those were not women at all. They were 'ladyboys', men who dress and behave as women."

The tradition is very ancient, and these people have their own caste – the Hijrah. In the time of the Raj, the British termed them hermaphrodites, neither male nor female. Some, but not all, are involved in the sex trade. Their presence, dancing and singing at birth or marriage ceremonies, can be auspicious and bestow blessings. Their curse is feared.

* * *

Our visit to Agra was not a great success. When we arrived, at about midnight, we spent some time standing around while poor Ashvini was bullied by the bus driver. He wanted payment for the seats occupied by our baggage, though there had been too few passengers to fill the bus and our bags were inside because the driver was unable to open the door of the luggage compartment. Eventually Ashvini resorted to calling headquarters, the disagreement was resolved, and a taxi called to take us to the hotel.

It was a slight improvement on the one in Delhi. But we were not allowed to sleep long because we were to visit the Taj Mahal at sunrise, when its beauty is revealed most dramatically. However, at seven o'clock in the morning it was bitterly cold, and the fog was so thick that we could not see the dome or the top of the minarets even when we had climbed the steps of the plinth on which the great monument stands. Our local guide kept telling us that the sun would soon clear the mist, but when it failed to appear he admitted that they had not seen the sun in Agra for the last four days.

We showed little interest in the souvenir shop into which our guide encouraged us. It was stocked with garish pictures, and alabaster plates inlaid with coloured stone. These were very inferior to the exquisite inlaid marble work I had seen the year before in the workshop of the family whose ancestors had decorated the Taj Mahal. We returned quickly to the hotel to have breakfast and get warm.

The breakfast room was clean and reasonably smart by European standards, but I looked out across the street to a big rubbish dump, where mangy dogs, a donkey and a large humped cow scavenged among the crows and egrets. A funeral procession came by, with the body, shrouded in white, carried on an open bier and followed by mourners – all men. I learnt later that women do not accompany their dead to the cremation, as they might weep and wail, which hinders the soul from leaving the body.

* * *

The sun began to appear as we left Agra (by the reasonably comfortable 'Government de luxe bus'), and we passed through the dramatic gap in the sandy cliffs that I remembered from the previous year to enter Jaipur as the sun set and a delicate crescent moon appeared in the twilight. Tina, Lena, Gabrielle and I stayed, for the three nights we spent in Jaipur, with a middle-aged couple,

Dr Kothari and his wife. What luxury! We shared two double en-suite bedrooms in their elegantly furnished house, and Mrs Kothari cooked us a delicious vegetarian dinner every evening. She and her husband had lived for some time in London, and both spoke excellent English. He watched *BBC World News* on the big wall-mounted television screen in the mornings.

Subhadra Kothari was described as a housewife on the information leaflet I had been given. Traditionally, Indian women become housewives when they marry and give up outside work. But women in rural areas do a lot of the farm work, and those of the lowest castes work with their husbands in backbreaking manual labour. Although these women are more than housewives, their work is not outside the family.

One of the girls who worked for the volunteer organisation told me that she was getting married in a few months' time, and when I asked her if she would continue to work for the organisation she answered, rather sadly I thought:

"No, when I marry I shall be just a housewife."

But Subhadra was not 'just a housewife'. She was an extremely good cook, and wrote a regular cookery column, as well as other articles, for a local newspaper. The following year, when I met her again, she told me she was starting to teach two courses, one on Hindi and the other on Indian cooking. I was to spend four weeks learning Hindi with her on my third trip to India as a volunteer.

Subhadra wore her dark hair short, and she was always beautifully and elegantly dressed in *salwar kameez* (trousers, long tunic and scarf) in soft autumnal colours, with a woollen jacket for warmth at this time of the year. The evening before we left she brought out her wedding dresses, made of heavy satin, embroidered in gold, and dressed us up in them. They were not saris but the long full skirts traditional to Rajasthan, worn with a bodice and the essential scarf. The dress for the actual wedding ceremony was pink, while on another day she had worn jade green.

* * *

Our three days in Jaipur were a hectic round of presentations at the volunteer headquarters and tourist excursions. In a room on the first floor, carpeted with mattresses covered in brightly patterned cloth, we heard talks on Indian life and culture, Hinduism and the caste system, the situation of women in India, and learnt a few useful phrases in Hindi. Those who arrived first sat at the back to lean against the wall, while later arrivals propped themselves up with cushions.

There was no trace of fog now, and the weather was warm and sunny. We ate lunch at tables on the flat roof of the headquarters building – rice, dal, vegetable curry and chapatis, with a banana or orange for dessert. I looked out over the parapet on a chaotic jumble of buildings, some painted white, others showing unadorned red brick or grey concrete. Gaily coloured laundry was hung to dry on some of the flat roofs. On others, people were engaged in household tasks, or sat sunning themselves.

The volunteer organisation runs a project to teach women from the slum area to make clothes. We visited the workshop where women were busy at old Singer sewing machines, some set on tables and others on the floor. A beautiful young woman squatted on the floor in front of one machine, dressed in tunic and trousers patterned in brilliant lime green and turquoise and working on a piece of shocking pink material. The supervisor produced cotton cloth in various colours and patterns, and several of us were measured for Indian-style *kurtas* and baggy trousers (to be delivered to us the following day). This *salwar kameez* is worn by many women. The outfit is completed with a matching scarf, worn draped below the neck in front, with the two ends thrown over the shoulders and hanging almost to the knees at the back.

We had not been there long before a group of children peered in at us from the doorway, and when Karin produced her camera they all wanted to be photographed. One of the older girls organised them into groups to pose for their pictures, smiling with delight, some of the smaller ones held in the arms of their older siblings. A couple of men appeared too and hung around. These were husbands, arriving to collect the money we were paying to their wives for our clothes. I hoped that the fact that their wives were contributing independently to the family income would raise their status in their husbands' eyes.

I had been warned before I left Ireland to dress conservatively in India. In the countryside it would be considered extremely indecent to show bare shoulders or legs, and even in Delhi and Jaipur, where some young women wore jeans and T-shirts, most women were wearing saris or *salwar kameez*. I never saw a cleavage or exposed shoulders or legs, except in photographs of Bollywood stars in the English-language *Times of India*. I chose to wear *salwar kameez*, which is elegant and comfortable. I found the scarf difficult to manage, and gave up wearing it while teaching as it tended to slide off my shoulders, but strictly speaking one is not properly dressed without it.

Some older women still wear the conventional red spot on their foreheads, indicating that they are married, but the *bindi* has become a fashion item. (*Bindi* literally means spot.) Stalls and shops sell plastic ones in all the colours of the rainbow, some embellished with shiny decoration, some round, others elongated. Girls and women wear them irrespective of their marital status, and choose one to suit their outfit. They are adhesive and can be worn on several occasions before the gum fails to work any longer.

* * *

One afternoon we were taken to a palatial cinema to see a Bollywood film. The big entrance hall was magnificent, with a sky blue ceiling spangled with gold stars, and cream and pink art-deco decorations round the lights on the wall. The huge auditorium was packed for the film. It was a comedy about three college friends, featuring plenty of singing and dancing, and of course a love interest.

A 'ragging' scene seemed to be inspired by behaviour in British public schools in the past. The new college students were subjected to bullying and demeaning treatment by the older ones. But I discovered that such behaviour occurs in some Indian colleges today. I saw ragging reported, and condemned, in *Times of India* articles.

The hero was forbidden to marry his sweetheart by her father, who disapproved of him. But in the end his friends rescued her from an arranged marriage in the middle of the wedding ceremony and transported her to the hero through the magnificent lake and mountain scenery of Ladakh. Audience participation was frequent and loud, and there was a great 'aah' of satisfaction when boy and girl were eventually reunited. (But they did not kiss – that would have been too indecent.)

* * *

We visited Jaipur's magnificent Amber Fort, riding up to it on elephants. Two at a time we climbed onto the seat strapped to an animal's back, and with its mahout sitting on its neck we lumbered slowly up the path which zig-zagged across the face of the rock on which the fort was perched.

The previous year we had been driven up by the access road. Amitabh had explained that his company no longer took tourists up on elephants because of a terrible accident. Elephants are very sensitive to fire and will trample out a flame. When a tourist took a flash photograph as he stood close to one animal it reacted as though there was a fire. It killed the tourist and then went mad and smashed its own mahout on the ground. Now there were notices forbidding photography close to the elephants, though many tourists ignored them. We were told that the elephants were rested after each ascent, and had their blood pressure and heart rate checked to make sure they were not stressed.

For me, the highlight of this excursion was to meet again the seller of perfumed oils, to whom I had been introduced by Amitabh the year before. I had taken a photo of him, and had brought a copy to give him. He was a tall handsome young man who recognised me immediately and greeted me with a big smile. He said many times in broken English that he was 'so pleased' to have the photo. There was no real shop, but his wares were displayed on the ledge of a small alcove in the wall of a covered way, which led up to the courtyard in front of the great Ganesh gate of the fort. His family had been selling their oils there for generations. I only had enough money with me to buy one vial of jasmine-scented oil, but as we were leaving the fort he came running after me with another small vial of perfumed oil as a gift.

* * *

We were to travel overnight by train to Barmer, a town fifty kilometres south of Shiv, where we would be picked up by the minibus from the volunteer camp. But once again the train was nearly five hours late, and we spent half the night at the station waiting for it. Most of us sat, cold and uncomfortable, on chairs in the 'Upper Class' waiting room, where the two benches were occupied by sleeping Japanese tourists. Caroline kept us entertained with amusing tales and photos she had taken in Jaipur, while Ashvini looked in every so often to say the train was an hour late, then two hours, then three…

The train finally arrived at half past four in the morning. An Indian girl kindly woke up long enough to help Lena, Caroline and me identify our bunks in the dark compartment to which Ashvini directed us. There was a blanket on my bunk which I pulled over myself, and with my rucksack as a pillow I fell immediately into a deep sleep.

When I woke and looked out of the window it was daylight and we were in the desert – a flat sandy landscape, where the few little trees had short knobbly branches which had been pollarded to provide firewood. The Indian girl who had helped us the night before spoke excellent English. She told us that she worked in Delhi and was coming home to her family in Jodhpur for the Constitution Day holiday.

A few hours beyond Jodhpur we reached Barmer and were met on the platform by Manoj from the volunteer camp at Shiv, who greeted us with:

"*Sabeko namaste* (Greetings to you all)."

We piled into a white minibus, our luggage was stacked on the roof, and we set off for the hour's drive northward through the Thar desert. For the next seven weeks I would be living in Shiv, far from the luxuries of Western civilisation, and working with children from one of the villages in this arid region.

Chapter 3

VOLUNTEERING IN SHIV

Shiv is a long narrow village straddling the big highway parallel to the Pakistani border, which runs roughly north-south in this region. The nearest towns are Barmer, fifty kilometres to the south, and Jaisalmer, a hundred kilometres to the north. All around lies the desert – that flat stony expanse, with a few low sandy hills on the horizon, which had captivated me on my first visit.

The volunteer camp, at the southern edge of the village, was a group of twenty or so thatched mud brick huts in a bare compound, enclosed by a low wall with a blue gate. Whenever the blue gate was left open, a couple of young cows would get in and stand in the shade of a hut, or join the crows and sparrows scavenging in the rubbish dump, until they were chased out by the staff.

My home was one of three huts arranged about a small courtyard, where I could sit and chat with others, or hang washing to dry. Two flowering bougainvillea bushes provided splashes of brilliant vermilion at the entrance to the courtyard, and when I had done my laundry I watered them from the bucket in which I had rinsed my clothes.

Little brown doves and collared doves cooed from the rooftops, and bright green bee-eaters perched on the electric wires. Every morning I watched bulbuls searching acrobatically for food in the branches of the single tall tree behind the dining hall. Apart from that tree, only a couple of little acacias and a few bushes managed to survive in the parched sandy ground. When the staff had done the laundry, the row of henna bushes beside the path to the dining hall bloomed with brightly patterned bedsheets spread out to dry.

We ate in the large hut which acted as kitchen and dining hall. There was always fresh fruit at lunch and dinner – bananas with more flavour than any I could buy at home, juicy little oranges, and occasionally a treat of fresh pineapple. Rinku, who worked in the kitchen, was kept busy for hours every day rolling out little circles of dough to make the chapatis which were served at every meal.

Our diet was similar to that of the locals – vegetable curries which always included potatoes, a lentil or chickpea dal and sometimes a tomato curry, always accompanied by rice and chapatis. Once a week a chicken curry interrupted this vegetarian regime, and occasionally we had eggs for breakfast. (Eggs are not considered vegetarian fare in India.) Some volunteers complained that the food lacked variety and was too high in carbohydrate. But it contained little fat, and no sugar except in the tea, and I soon became fitter and slimmer than I had been for years.

Outside the back of the dining hall after meals we washed our metal plates and cups with poisonous-looking bright blue soap in a big stone sink, shaded from the sun by a canopy of thatch. Crows perched on the red hanging bucket where we disposed of food scraps. Further back, away from the huts, was the rubbish dump, marked out by a low wall two or three bricks high. The staff burnt the rubbish once during my seven weeks there. Nearby was a heap of unused bricks where two of the little striped squirrels lived. The other non-human inhabitants of the compound were several thin stray dogs, including a bitch with three tiny puppies. We were asked not to encourage them by feeding them, but I saw some of the Indian staff secretly giving them chapatis.

I kept in touch with family and friends at home through email, as there were two computers for our use in the hut which served as an office. We relaxed or prepared lessons in the recreation hall, another large hut carpeted with brightly coloured mattresses. Previous volunteers had left a stock of books and posters which I mined for teaching material. In the evening before it grew dark, Indian staff and volunteers played volleyball on the sandy ground between the office and recreation hall.

I grew to love my little thatched hut. The mosquito net over the bed was unnecessary – there were no mosquitos at this time of year, and my resident geckos were very efficient at keeping down the insect life. I had never realised before that geckos could make a noise, but these chittered as one chased the other round the wall.

At one end of the hut a door opened into the bathroom, with a Western-style toilet and a small sink with a mirror over it. Cold water came from the black plastic tank on the bathroom roof, but hot water had to be collected from a communal tap outside one of the huts. I rapidly became converted to bucket showers – pouring hot water over myself from a bucket using a plastic jug – and did not miss the European variety at all. One day when I went to fetch hot water the two cows were standing in the shade nearby. As soon as I turned on the tap they came and pushed me out of the way and stuck their heads into my bucket. But they soon realised the water was too hot to drink and retired to their place in the shade.

The solar panels on poles around the camp had ceased to work, but the electricity supply from the Rajasthani grid was reasonably dependable. It rarely failed for more than a few minutes at a time, unlike the power supplies I discovered later elsewhere. It was probably the military presence in this strategic border area that ensured both a good electricity supply and the excellent maintenance of the main road.

Water, on the other hand, was scarce. Frequently one of the black plastic tanks on the bathroom roofs would run dry, and then there would be calls of "*Pani, pani* (Water, water)." One of the staff would climb up on the roof with a green garden hose to refill it from the main water tank behind the kitchen.

It was chilly in the mornings, and I needed my fleece jacket. Morning *chai* was provided half an hour before breakfast – tea brewed up with milk, sugar and spices. A group of us would drink it sitting on the step outside the office hut, basking like lizards in the morning sun. *Chai* was served in the afternoon as well. This morning and afternoon tea habit must have been inherited from the British, like the game of cricket, and both have become part of the Indian way of life.

Cricket is as popular in India as soccer is at home, although officially their national game is hockey. Wherever there is a bare patch of land, local lads will play cricket, with any available stick for a bat and a variety of objects standing in for wickets. When I asked Ashvini if there was any interesting news in the Hindi-language newspaper that he read every day, he would always give me the latest cricket scores.

* * *

After breakfast on Constitution Day everyone in the camp congregated in front of the recreation hall, where a flagpole had been erected. At its foot a map of India had been drawn in coloured chalk on the sandy ground and covered with red bougainvillea flowers. Rinku, the only woman on the staff, was asked to raise the flag, which scattered more petals as it unfurled. Then the staff sang the national anthem, distributed little sweets made of milk and sugar, and the camp manager (whom we called Manoj-ji to distinguish him from the other Manoj) told us about the Indian Republic and its Constitution.

"The Constitution of India came into force on 26th January 1950," he said. "India had become independent in 1947. The Constitution is written in Hindi and English, and declares India to be a sovereign, socialist, secular, democratic republic, with a president and parliamentary government."

Many Indians knew little about Ireland, and so I would explain to them that, like India, it was partitioned when the south became independent from Britain, and the Republic was declared in 1948, just over a year before India adopted its own constitution and officially became a republic.

I knew that, at partition, Pakistan was created as a Muslim country. But reading a little about Indian history I discovered that Mahatma Gandhi and Jawaharlal Nehru (the first prime minister) had always had the vision of India as a state without any particular religious affiliation, and so the word 'secular' was inserted in the constitution. Unfortunately this does not mean that violence never breaks out between Hindus and Muslims living in India.

When I moved to Ireland the Troubles in the North were becoming violent again, and there was anti-British sentiment among the general public in the South. But in India the days of the Raj seem to have been confined to history. An Irish historian remarked to me:

"The Indians have forgiven the British. The Irish still have not."

In India I never encountered anything but friendly interest when I admitted to being English. I was warned, however, that in some rural areas people were still resentful of white-skinned people, identifying them all as British.

As I learnt about India's history I found it surprising that it had succeeded in becoming, and remaining, a democracy (apart from the years from 1975-77 when Prime Minister Indira Gandhi declared a State of Emergency and cancelled elections).

"Britain gave India democracy," said one of the other volunteers.

"But in that case, why are all other countries in Africa and Asia which were part of the British Empire not democratic?" I replied.

The British did not govern the empire democratically. They ruled the Indian princely states through the local maharajas, and these states were far from democratic. Nor, in the areas of direct British rule, were Indians given the vote or introduced to democratic procedures.

However, the British did promote education, and eventually began to allow educated Indians to play more of a part in the Indian civil service and the courts of law. Many of those who became prominent in the independence movement, such as Gandhi and Nehru, had studied law and been called to the Bar in England. I believe the fact that India is a democracy today must be largely due to their determination that independent India should be a democratic state.

* * *

My daily journey to school remains a vivid memory. The minibus turns off the main road onto a sandy track westwards into the desert. At first it winds between bushes and one or two big trees, and then it sets off across a featureless expanse. There is no marked road, and I wonder how the driver chooses one route rather than another through the tangle of tyre tracks in the sand. Soon a couple of electricity pylons appear on the horizon, and beyond them the little white houses of the village, the small square temple, and a slightly larger building painted pink (the colour of government buildings) which is the school. As the minibus draws near, the children run to meet us, barefoot, with bright eyes and smiling faces. Most of them wear school uniform – short navy skirts and white blouses for the girls and fawn shorts or trousers with sky blue shirts for the boys. Their clothes are rather worn and faded but they are always clean.

The school consisted of a single room for the thirty or so children and their teacher. Alex, Joya and I divided the children into three groups and sat with them in different corners of the room. Joya took the babies' class, for five- to six-year-olds, but she always had a few younger children as well who had followed their older brothers and sisters and were allowed to stay. One of them was a toddler, not yet two years old, who was a bit of a nuisance as he ate the crayons and distracted the others. Alex had classes II and III, ranging in age from six to eight years old, and my nine- to eleven-year-olds were in classes IV and V. (It amused me to discover that the classes in Indian primary schools were identified by Roman numerals.)

The children sat on mats on the floor, and Alex and I each had a blackboard propped up against the wall behind us. Volunteers had painted the schoolroom white and decorated it in bright colours with the letters of the Roman alphabet, the numbers from one to twenty, and a picture of a tree with pink flowers. In an alcove next to my blackboard was a framed picture of Saraswati, Goddess of Knowledge and the Arts, holding a book and a pen in two of her four hands, while with the other pair she played a musical instrument that looked like a very long-necked lute. She was seated on a lotus with a swan gliding beside her.

One of the Indian staff from the camp accompanied us to school as our 'executive', to help and translate if necessary. We were lucky to have Mr Narula, who was a retired schoolteacher and could tell us about the primary school curriculum and give excellent and authoritative help with planning and delivering lessons. After the first couple of weeks he was transferred to assist new volunteers at another school, but by this time we were more confident. He was replaced by Manoj, who was in his twenties like most of the executives, and later still by Ashvini.

The schoolteacher did not speak much English (through Mr Narula he explained that he had studied Sanskrit as his main subject at college). But he would come over and explain to the children when I failed to make myself understood. He had asked for volunteers and took an interest in what we were doing. Some volunteers at other schools complained that the teachers left the class when they arrived, and sat outside reading or chatting. Once a teacher has been appointed to a government school they have a job for life which is well-paid (by Indian standards), and some treat it as a sinecure.

On some days, when we arrived a little early, school prayers were still in progress, so we waited outside on the veranda. The children stood in two or three lines in front of the picture of Saraswati and chanted a long prayer to her, ending with '*Shanti, shanti, shanti* (Peace, peace, peace)'. They finished by singing the national anthem, and then they were ready to stand in a big circle to sing the 'Good Morning Song' (to the tune of 'Frère Jacques'):

Say good morning, say good morning,
How are you, how are you?
Time to start the lesson, time to start the lesson,
Now now now, now now now.

When my class had come to sit cross-legged on the mat in front of me I would take the attendance register. As I called a name, that child would jump to his or her feet and say "Yes ma'am". Then I would ask, "What day is it today?" and one or more of them would shout out the answer, some in English and some in Hindi. Pratap, one of the older boys, loved to stand up and recite the days of the week in English, and then the others would take it in turns to do the same.

Their English was rudimentary but they enjoyed reading the words on the flash cards I held up. They recognised 'sun', 'cat', 'dog' and even 'queen', without seeing the picture on the other side of the card, and they eagerly identified shapes, birds or wild animals on the posters I brought from the stock of teaching aids in the recreation hall at camp. I taught them to identify the countries where animals on the posters lived – 'tiger lives in India', 'cheetah lives in Africa' (for some reason the cheetah was their favourite animal) – and showed them those places on the inflatable globe I had brought with me. As soon as they saw the globe they would point to the blue oceans and shout excitedly, "*Pani, pani.*" They had probably never seen a stretch of water larger than the small pond in Shiv which was the local water supply.

They were so keen to learn. Little Suresh, who was one of the less able, would look at me with big bright eyes wanting desperately to answer a question correctly. Sangita was the cleverest child in the school. She was always first to finish the writing I had given them, and did it very neatly, although it was not easy for them to write well leaning over their papers on the floor. Pratap and Rakesh were also very bright, especially at Maths. Most of them added numbers by drawing a set of vertical dashes to represent each number and counting the total number of dashes. Others counted on their fingers – not in the way I expected, but by counting each knuckle. So with three knuckles on each finger and two on each thumb they could reach a total of twenty-eight rather than the ten we reach by counting fingers and thumbs. They learnt Maths through Hindi with their teacher, but it was essential for them to learn to do it in English as well. My class could all count in English up to a hundred, but found it difficult to hear the difference between numbers such as thirty and thirteen.

These children spoke a dialect of Rajasthani as their mother tongue. Rajasthani, and the languages of most of the northern and central states, are Indo-European, like Hindi. But languages in the south are completely different. There is at least one local language in every state in India. Hindi, which is derived from the ancient Sanskrit, is the official language of central government, according to the constitution, though only a very small minority speak Hindi as their first language. English is also an official language and is used in the Supreme and High Courts of law. In the north, the teaching in government schools is through Hindi. However, English provides access to well-paid jobs, and many private schools teach through English.

As soon as they start school here in the north of India, children learn both Hindi and English. That means learning two completely different alphabets, our Roman one and the Devanagari one in which Hindi is written, which has over forty letters. My class were proficient (as far as I could tell) at reading and writing Hindi. When I introduced a new English word I would tell them what it meant in Hindi, and Sangita or Pratap would come up and write the Hindi word on the board next to the English one. Irish children have a comparatively easy time, learning only one new language when they start school and using only the Roman alphabet. Most never become bilingual in English and Irish, but these Indian children must be able to communicate in Hindi as well as their own local language. So they are at least bilingual, and those who attend private schools which teach through English will be trilingual.

There was a huge innocence about this teaching environment, so different from a school at home. Was this what the ancient hedge schools in Ireland were like? In spite of the lack of facilities and teaching aids, the children were being given a basic education, and they loved school. But how many of them would be able to continue beyond class V? The girls were destined to be housewives, and a good education was not a priority for them or their families. The men of the village were all carpenters, and their sons would be expected to follow them in the trade. While education up to the age of fourteen might be useful to them it would not be vital for their livelihoods. They would learn their craft from their fathers, or carpenters in another village.

* * *

During break the teacher coached the older boys in cricket. They were good at throwing overarm, and he was teaching them to bowl properly. We always brought the cricket bat and ball from the camp, and also skipping ropes and marbles for the children to play with.

After break we played games and sang songs in English. All the children stood round in a big circle to sing, with appropriate hand motions, 'Twinkle, Twinkle, Little Star', or 'Head, Shoulders, Knees and Toes'. Then they would clamour for 'Simon Says'. It took a while to get across the idea that if a command does not start with 'Simon says' then they should not obey it, and some never became very good at noticing the difference. They also liked to play a game in which they sat round in a circle with their hands out touching those of the child on either side. The children called out the days of the week in turn round the circle, tapping the hand of the next child as they spoke. When it reached 'Sunday' there was a scramble for the next child to escape being tapped. Successful evasion resulted in the child who had spoken being 'out' . Otherwise the tapped child was out.

They were never jealous of the winner of any of these games, and all applauded at the end. Nor did they fight. They might push one another around a bit in play, but there never seemed to be a real display of anger or aggression. I believe it was the influence of their teacher, whom they called their guru. He was always gentle and kind, and he never slapped them.

After the songs and games I would hand out paper and crayons to my class. They always drew flowers and peacocks, stars and hearts, and would ask me to draw dogs, camels or elephants for them. Then it was time for the 'Goodbye Song', again to the tune of 'Frère Jacques':

Say goodbye now, say goodbye now,
Time to go, time to go,
See you in the morning, see you in the morning,
Bye bye bye, bye bye bye.

The minibus would arrive to take us back to camp, and the teacher would be left to give the children their lunch and take the whole school for lessons for the rest of the day.

* * *

When it was time for Alex and Joya to leave Shiv, we visited some of the homes in the village where we taught. All the children accompanied us as we walked round, and their mothers veiled their faces with their long scarves as we approached. Younger wives did not cover their faces, but refused to be photographed. One fifteen-year-old girl was back home from her husband's village, to visit her family while he was away learning carpentry. Although the legal minimum age for marriage in India is eighteen for girls and twenty-one for boys, it is traditional in Rajasthan for girls to be married younger, and many are wives at fourteen or fifteen. Even the practice of child marriage has not completely disappeared.

Each of the low flat-roofed houses had an outer courtyard, with a kitchen area in one corner covered by a piece of corrugated iron roofing. Some households owned a cow, which was kept in another corner of the courtyard, shaded by thatch. There were some circular concrete structures, which were the tops of water tanks, but as the villagers had to pay for these to be filled by a water tanker I would often see women with shining metal pots on their heads walking across the desert to collect water from the pond at Shiv six or seven kilometres away.

The mud brick houses of the original village had been washed away when the monsoon rains had reached into the desert several years earlier. An international NGO had built sixteen new houses and a community hall in stone on this new site, which was on slightly higher ground a little way from the original village. The villagers had offered the hall to the government for use as a primary school. There were no shops or stalls, but the villagers were using building material, which had been left in small piles around the place, to build more houses.

The first thing they had built for themselves was a little temple, and there was a festival in my second week there when it was inaugurated. Relatives from other places came to stay. This boosted the numbers in school, as visiting children would join our classes – not because they were made to, but because they wanted to. One day two of my girls were not present until after break because their new house was being blessed. When they turned up they were wearing beautiful *salwar kameez*, one in pink, the other in turquoise – clearly their best clothes.

On one of the houses the NGO had left an inscription in Hindi which read, in translation, 'The low status of women is due to illiteracy'. Half my class were girls, but the chance of them continuing their education beyond the age of eleven or twelve was very small. When I asked the teacher if Sangita would go on to another school next year, he answered regretfully that it was unlikely. She would need the support of the village – not financial support, as the state has enshrined in the constitution the right of all children between the ages of six and fourteen to free education. However, the villagers did not see the need for a girl to be educated beyond class V. She was likely to be married by the time she was fifteen, and become a housewife, helping her mother-in-law in her husband's family home in another village.

I had two eleven-year-old girls in my class, but they did not often come to school. When one of them joined the class one morning, her aunt (who looked scarcely older than herself) came along shortly afterwards and took her away to herd the goats.

* * *

We took it for granted that there were roughly as many girls as boys in the school and the village. But Lena and I discovered that, even in the recent past, this was not necessarily the normal state of affairs. One weekend we were in Jaisalmer and took the opportunity to have an Ayurvedic massage. As we were leaving, a group of half a dozen young women came in, and the masseuse introduced them.

"This girl is going to be married soon, and these are her friends," she said. "She will be a very special bride. She is the first girl in her village to be married for a hundred years." Then she added, "All the other girls died. But things are better now, and there are several young girls living in her village."

At first I did not understand, but then I realised she meant that, for a century, girl children in that village had not survived to marriageable age. They had been neglected or starved, or even killed at birth.

Traditionally, boy children are preferred. Girls must be provided with an expensive dowry, and when a girl marries she moves to her husband's family home and is no longer a help to her own family. Female infanticide has skewed the sex ratio. The number of women in India was only ninety-four to every hundred men in 2011[2], compared with the Western world in which there are slightly more women than men (around 101 women to 100 men). In India foetal sex determination has been banned, and I was told that the abortion of a female foetus is illegal. But those who can afford to pay can procure sex determination and abortion services. The sex imbalance has now become worse in the cities than in rural areas.

But it would be wrong to think that all Indians want sons and not daughters. Many men I talked to were proud of their daughters. On a camel safari the following year, the man in charge of my camel was delighted with his first baby, a girl, and insisted on showing me photos of her on his mobile phone as he rode

---

2 The Indian census results are a mine of information. On the sex ratio see http://www.census2011.co.in/sexratio.php.

behind me. A teacher at one of the schools where I taught had one daughter and told me he did not want a son, and several people said, "One son and one daughter make a complete family."

* * *

Shiv village was a ten-minute walk along the main road from the volunteer camp. We passed three tall communication masts in the compound next to the camp, and a few little houses spaced well apart on either side of the road. The intervals between houses decreased until we entered the bustle of Shiv itself.

Once, on the way back to camp, almost opposite the compound with the communication masts, I saw a black goat giving birth to a kid. Its owner was on hand to help the little thing stand when it collapsed, and the mother licked it and nudged it towards her udder. Just outside the camp I found one of the puppies lying dead by the roadside, with crows feeding on it. *This is India,* I thought *– life and death, the mediaeval and the modern, side by side. It is like living in a cross-section of time.*

Shiv was much bigger than the village where I taught in the mornings, with stalls lining the sandy verges of the main road, and shops behind them. A ramshackle plank bridged a ditch in front of the shops. The ground was littered with paper, cartons, plastic bags and other more unsavoury rubbish. But the fruit and vegetables set out for sale looked fresh and clean, and very colourful – little purple aubergines, white cauliflowers and green cabbages, pink onions, green peppers, deep red carrots, oranges, green grapes and small yellow bananas.

Other stalls sold soft drinks, biscuits and crisps; there was an array of shiny metal buckets and bowls outside one shop, and another displayed brightly coloured hanks of rope; a tiny shack was stacked with multicoloured packs of old saris, to be recycled into patchwork cushion covers and quilts. Shops selling toothpaste, soap, shampoo and moisturising creams stocked many European brands. Near the far end of the village, metal tools and utensils were carefully arranged on a large sheet spread on the ground. They were all recycled from metal parts of old lorries. Razor-sharp shears and scissors were made of the hard steel from axles.

There was usually a traffic jam of buses, army lorries and tractors, with goats and cows wandering in the road to add to the chaos. Shiv boasted a police station, painted pink, and a post office, as well as an ATM. On the first day that we arrived we were taken to the police station to be registered, and we had to visit it again to sign out when we left at the end of our time there. Only eighty kilometres of desert separate Shiv from the Pakistani border, and all this area is a restricted zone. During the winter the Indian army holds manoeuvres in the region, before the weather gets too hot. There were often army personnel in the village, and as the minibus drove us to school I saw camps of camouflaged tents in the desert.

Early one morning in mid February all of us in the volunteer camp were woken by a big explosion, and the earth shook a little. It was clear that it was a bomb, and it caused consternation among the volunteers – was this the start of a border skirmish? But there were no further explosions, and the panic gradually subsided.

Later that morning Bengt met a young soldier in Shiv village who, in response to his query, said:

"We didn't do anything – it was another platoon."

He added that thousands of troops were withdrawing from the area.

That afternoon army lorries started to move off southward. A huge transporter, carrying a tank camouflaged with leafy branches, was stopped by a puncture on the roadside opposite the camp. The next week the camouflaged tents in the desert had all disappeared.

The police station was a walled enclosure, with a forecourt shaded by one or two trees, and inside the building was cool and airy. We sat on chairs, while the executive with us gave our names and nationalities to a policeman in khaki uniform sitting at one of the desks. An old rifle with fixed bayonet was propped up in a corner. No modern weapons were to be seen. On one wall was a big map labelled 'Crime Map 2006'. Had there been no crime worth recording in the three years since then? Lock-ups inside the outer wall of the compound looked dilapidated and unused, and there was a pair of rusty handcuffs hanging outside one of them.

* * *

The tailor's shop stood on a little street off the main road, with three wooden steps leading up to a long narrow room. Before afternoon classes we would sit on the bench along one side, or the plastic chairs opposite it, to chat and drink the *chai* the tailor brought us. Brightly coloured material hung on wooden rods and strings along the walls, ready to be made up into *kurtas* and trousers. Some of the finished products hung beside them on hangers, waiting to be collected. At the back, bottles of fizzy drinks were arrayed on shelves and on top of a small fridge. Shelves near the front held packets of sweets, balls and kites, pens, pencils and rubbers, and all sorts of trinkets.

It was to the tailor that we went when we needed our mobile phones topped up, and he provided bus tickets for our weekend trips to Jaisalmer. It was actually his wife who made the clothes. (As their daughter said, "It's not really my father who is the tailor, it's my mother.") She also sewed parcels into the white cotton covers required by the postal service. When I was finally leaving Shiv I was unable to pack everything into my suitcase, so the tailor found me a cardboard box to pack the excess in, and his wife shrouded it in white cotton. I dispatched it from the post office, and to my surprise it reached home before I did.

A sandy unpaved street parallel to the main road was a residential area, where the newer houses were built of stone. A green patch of garden beside one house contrasted sharply with the arid surroundings. Someone must have made sure the vegetables and flowers growing there were well watered.

Further along this street there was a temple with a tall white tower, which I saw from the main road on the way to school every morning. A young man offered to take us there. He taught at one of the private secondary schools in Shiv and was keen to practise his English.

"I am twenty-two," he said, "and I am the principal of the school. I have one hundred and fifty pupils."

Three teenage boys who were his pupils tagged along. A bronze bell hung at the entrance to a small temple beside the large white one.

"Take off your shoes," our guide told us, "and ring the bell. It will call the attention of the God."

It was dark inside and unlit. But the inner sanctum of the white temple, into which we peered through a mesh door, was gaudily decorated with bright green lights. There were steps going down to a cellar, and our guide said:

"Down there is the place where the God manifested himself."

It happened during a festival, celebrated with drumming and dancing far into the night, he explained. On such occasions the drumming becomes mesmerising and the dancing frenzied. Then one of the dancers may enter a trancelike state in which the god enters him.

* * *

A cement mixer was pouring its load into a large pit beside the main road, and the cement was disappearing down a wide vertical hole in the centre. A man at the top, who seemed to be in charge, spoke English and was keen to explain what was going on.

"This is a pipeline to bring water from the Punjab to the desert," we were told.

The last of the cement was scraped down with a piece of card, and we saw that there were men inside a large pipe at the bottom of the hole.

"The water pipe is metal," said the man in charge, "so the men in the pipe have a machine to coat it inside with cement. Otherwise the water will rust it."

Punjab means 'Land of the five rivers', though, as the Punjab is divided between India and Pakistan, not all of them are in Indian territory. However, there is a lot of water in the Indian Punjab, hundreds of kilometres to the north-east of arid Rajasthan.

The existing Shiv water supply was a small pond, a little way back from the main road over a low hill. Black and white stilts with long red legs stalked in the water, and a little brown pond heron squatted at the edge. Water tankers towed by tractors were filled up here, to supply other villages. Before I left they were supplying the camp, too, after lightning damaged the electric pump which filled the main water tank automatically.

There was yet another small temple next to the pond. Women in colourful saris visited it, and a few children begged outside. This was the only place in Shiv where I ever saw anyone begging.

* * *

One week the children in Shiv were vaccinated against polio. Lena, who was a nurse, Alex, and Hitesh (one of the executives) helped a district nurse. On the first day parents brought their children to a vaccination centre set up in a school. At home we give the oral vaccine on a lump of sugar, but here the nurse held the child and opened its mouth, while Lena squeezed in two drops of the vaccine. Then Alex painted the fifth fingernail on the child's right hand black to show it had been vaccinated, and Hitesh filled in the official record sheet.

The next day Lena and the nurse took one section of the village and visited every house. They vaccinated any children who had not attended the previous day's session, and marked in chalk on the outside of the house the date of the visit and how many children had been found there and vaccinated. When they met a small child in the street the nurse checked its fingernail, and if it was not marked she held the child while Lena dropped the vaccine into its mouth. This must have been terrifying for the child.

Lena had taken photos of some of the children she had vaccinated, and the tailor had had them printed for her. I went with her one afternoon to take one of her photos to a family on the edge of Shiv village, where she had given a three-month-old baby the vaccine. When we arrived, the baby's grandfather and father were feeding their cow. The animal was tethered in a thatched corner of their outer courtyard, and they were picking fresh bright green grass for it from a small cultivated area. We showed them the photo, and they stopped what they were doing and invited us into an inner courtyard, pulling down a *palang* (a bed consisting of a wooden frame criss-crossed with rope) for us to sit on.

The women and children all gathered round to greet us – the grandmother, her daughter-in-law with the baby and a two-year-old son, and two married daughters who were visiting, each with a young daughter. The grandmother and her daughters did not cover their faces (there was no male executive accompanying us) but the daughter-in-law veiled her face in the presence of her father-in-law.

The two-year-old boy could not stand by himself, and his grandfather, who spoke a little English, explained that the child had had very weak muscles ever since he was born.

"Doctors say he must exercise a lot," he said.

He stood the child where he could hold onto the *palang* and told him, in English, to sit down and then stand up. The child clearly understood the English, though he found it hard to perform the actions.

The baby was lying on a mat on another *palang*, his eyes rimmed with black kohl to keep away the evil eye. The old man was clearly very proud and fond of all his grandchildren, and I took a photo of him with the smaller girl and the two-year-old boy in his arms, with the older girl standing beside him.

The women brewed *chai* for us on a stove in the corner and offered us savoury deep-fried pastries. They had recently re-surfaced the courtyard with a preparation of mud, which dried to give a very hard sandy-brown finish. Then they had painted colourful patterns on it – green and yellow stars inside white geometric shapes with sun-like rays. This was in preparation for the festival of Holi.

* * *

My schoolchildren out in the desert were very poor. When we instituted a toothbrushing session after break every day, their teacher explained that their families could not afford to buy toothpaste. In contrast, the girls at my afternoon English and Computing class in Shiv itself came from better-off families, with shops or businesses in the village. These girls attended fee-paying private schools.

The volunteer organisation had arranged to use a room in the tailor's own house for the lessons and had provided two computers. These occupied a bench below a shelf supporting a television set, and there was a plastic chair in front of each and a couch with cushions along the wall at the side. The room was rather dark as there were no windows, and daylight entered only through the door opening onto the courtyard.

As there were sometimes ten girls in the class, ranging in age between ten and fourteen years, Alex and I took two at a time to work at the computers, while Lena taught English to the rest outside in the courtyard. They sat on a mat in front of a blackboard attached to the wall. Hitesh, our executive, shared his time between the three of us. After Alex had gone back to America, Hitesh joined me teaching at the computers. Occasionally the power would fail, on a couple of occasions for as long as half an hour, and then we would all join in the English lesson outside until it came back on again.

The girls were better at English than the children I taught in the mornings. Lena had them reading in turn from a book and then answering questions to check that they had understood what they read. We found that fairy tales such as *Ali Baba and the Forty Thieves* or *Cinderella* were the most successful. They were less culturally biased than most of the European stories we found in the recreation hall, so the girls related to them better.

There was no internet connection to the computers, so we taught them to use MS Word and gave them practice in writing English at the same time. They wrote short essays about themselves and their friends, their school day and what they did in their holidays. Apparently their best friends were all beautiful, with long dark hair, and liked chocolate. Kesar, who was fourteen, had a best friend who wore jeans and a T-shirt, but she told me that she herself preferred Indian dress. She was always beautifully turned out in a different *salwar kameez* every day, and she commented one day, pointing to my *kurta*:

"The same as yesterday."

So I felt the need to buy some more clothes, to live up to her expectations.

The grandmother of the house, and one or two of the girls' mothers, would sit on a low wall opposite the blackboard to watch the lessons. Kanta and Sangita's mother was often there with their young brother. She spoke English and was inclined to help the girls answer Lena's questions. Sometimes the tailor's wife would bring us *chai* flavoured with ginger, and tasty little pastries. These women did not veil their faces, even in front of

Alex and Hitesh. When the lesson ended the girls would insist on singing the 'Goodbye Song' and shaking hands all round. I would say "*Namaste*" to the grandmother and the mothers sitting on the wall, putting my hands together and bowing slightly in the appropriate manner, and the tailor's wife would come out from her sewing to say goodbye.

* * *

The houses where these girls lived in Shiv were very different from those in the village where my school was. Although the tailor's house had an open courtyard in front, the kitchen was not outside but just inside the building. Other houses opened directly onto the street and had smart front doors.

One afternoon after class Kesar invited me to her house. It was a big new stone building, with at least six rooms, two of them really large. Her mother and two sisters greeted me, and Kesar proudly showed me round. There was an array of beautifully bright and shiny metal cups, pots and plates on shelves in one room, and toys and pictures on shelves in another. But in spite of this relative luxury the furnishings were sparse. *Palangs* were tipped up against the wall in bedrooms. Kesar brought out a plastic chair for me to sit on in the main room, which was furnished with mats and cushions on the floor and a television set. She offered me *ladoo* (a sweet made from milk and sugar) which her mother had made.

Another day Lali grabbed my hand and insisted that I visit her home. It was on the corner near the tailor's shop, and we went in through an ornate ironwork front door. Just inside I met her brother, about ten or eleven years old, with two of his friends. But Lali dragged me on through another room and out of a door opening onto a big grassy area. To the left was another part of the house, with a courtyard in front.

Lots of Lali's relations were assembled there. I said "*Namaste*" to them all, and Lali pointed to one after another – "my uncle", "my aunt", "my sister", "my mother", "my grandmother". There were several aunts and uncles and some small cousins. The grandmother, mother and older sister were engaged in some beautiful embroidery, which I admired. One of the uncles spoke a little English and asked me to take photos of them all. Then another young woman appeared and he said, "No photo." I did not discover why she was different. None of the women were veiled, but perhaps she should have been.

* * *

Hitesh and I often walked back to camp after the afternoon class. He had a master's degree in tourism and wanted to become an international tourist guide. Working with volunteers gave him the opportunity to improve his fluency in English. He started calling me *dadi-ji*, meaning grandmother (on the father's side; the mother's mother is *nani-ji*). At first I objected, but I soon realised that he did not mean it in a derogatory way, and so I called him *pota* (grandson). The young Indians I met had more respect for older people than I was used to at home. Perhaps as a consequence of living in an extended family, often with three generations in one house, they had no difficulty in relating to older people and talking with them, as well as being extremely good with young children.

Hitesh explained that I reminded him of his grandmother because of the way I had my hair pinned up. He had clearly been very fond of her. He told me that she had worked at home making clothes as part of a cottage industry.

"The family was very poor, and there were times when she found it hard to put food on the table for them," he said.

She had had five daughters and three sons. Hitesh's father had left the family home when he married and, through persistence and hard work, had built up a good business making metal water pots and was respected in the community.

As I got to know him better, Hitesh confided in me that he had fallen in love with a European girl and wanted to marry her. But he had not yet dared to tell his parents about her. He was the youngest son in his family and the only child who had gone on to higher education. All his brothers and cousins worked in Udaipur where the family lived, most of them in the family business. Two of his married brothers (whose marriages had, of course, been arranged) lived in the family home with their wives and the young son of one of them. Hitesh's parents found it hard to understand why he was working away from home, on a relatively small salary, and would have been appalled at the thought of him choosing his own wife, let alone a foreigner.

Hitesh told me how much he wanted to be able to make use of his training and his ability with languages. He hoped that if he got a job as an international tourist guide, with a good salary, his parents would think he was making a success of his life and be more prepared to accept a foreign daughter-in-law. He realised that living in the family home would be impossible for a European girl, and he wanted to be able to set up house with his girlfriend on their own. She was still in third-level education, so they could not think of getting married before she finished her course.

One evening Hitesh called me out of my hut to talk, and we sat outside on the office steps in the warm dark. He was very upset because his sister-in-law had told him that his parents wanted to find him a wife. They were planning to arrange a marriage for his younger sister, who would be eighteen on her next birthday, and they wanted it to be a double wedding. He still felt he could not tell them about his girlfriend, but was determined to refuse an arranged marriage.

* * *

My hut had a small gap in the centre of the thatch, and on some mornings I was woken by the cheeping of sparrows that had managed to get in through it. But early one morning I was woken by a most unexpected sound – the drumming of rain on the thatched roof and on the hard sand of the courtyard outside. I had been vaguely aware of thunder and lightning, but the rain jolted me awake. No sooner had I wondered when it would start to drip through the hole in the roof than it stopped. Outside, the washing hung up to dry was damp, and there were little pools of water on the plastic chairs. Fantastic cloud formations were lit by the rising sun. But there was no more rain.

The only other time there was any humidity in the air was one Monday, when the sky was completely overcast. A wind whipped up the sand outside the school, and in the afternoon one or two drops of moisture – you could hardly call it rain – fell on my English and Computing class. The girls got very excited and pointed at the sky. They asked:

"When is the monsoon in Ireland?" and I replied:

"All year."

By supper time the sky was beginning to clear, and the sun set, staining towering clouds red.

The nights became very cold one week in February – only a few degrees above zero. There was a bitter wind during the day, and we sat to chat in the courtyard outside our huts huddled in fleeces and blankets. Very early, on one of the coldest mornings, there was a great snuffling and scuffling outside, and I discovered that one of the dogs was making himself comfortable and warm in the blankets we had left on a *palang*. We were told that it was snowing at the volunteer camp in Himachal Pradesh, and the Hindi-language newspaper that the executives read showed a photo of the Capitol in Washington DC covered in the deepest snow for a hundred and ten years.

After that the weather got steadily warmer. By late February it was too hot for the children to play outside at break, and instead they played the 'days of the week' game, and 'statues', in the schoolroom. Soon it was reaching forty degrees in the middle of the day. I started taking a siesta after lunch, before going to Shiv for my afternoon class with the girls. The air was so dry that, however hot it became, I was never sticky. The mud brick walls of my hut insulated me from the heat, and although I had an electric fan I did not often need to use it.

The sight of sheep looking as though they had been given rather rough crew cuts heralded the shearing season. I saw huge lorries overloaded with packs of wool, which bulged over their sides and almost scraped the road at the rear. A large iron scales was set up beside the road at one end of Shiv village. Lorries would empty their packs onto the ground, open at the top so that the wool overflowed onto the sand, and it was weighed on the scales before being repacked and dispatched to be processed.

In mid March the school hours changed to their summer schedule, starting two hours earlier, at eight o'clock, so that the children could be at home in the shade during the heat of the afternoon. In mid April the volunteer camp would close altogether because of the heat, and the school holidays would begin in mid May and continue until the monsoon arrived in Rajasthan in July. Although it did not often bring rain to the desert (and there had been a complete drought in this region for the last three years) it brought cooler air.

* * *

The tailor served us *chai* while we waited in his shop for the bus to Jaisalmer. Lena, Bengt and I were going there for the weekend. We got a little anxious as the time that the bus was due approached, but the tailor said:

"Don't worry. I will be told when it is coming."

Quarter of an hour later his phone rang, and he ushered us out to the main road, where the bus duly stopped, and waved us off. (He was waiting when we arrived back in Shiv the following evening, and boarded our bus to tell the driver to take us on as far as the camp gates.)

The bus had a driver, a conductor, and a little boy (the son or younger brother of one of them) who leaned perilously out of the door as we approached every stop and shouted:

"Jaisalmer, Jaisalmer."

We were treated to a background of Rajasthani music, and the driver sounded his horn loudly whenever he overtook sheep or goats on the road, and each time he neared a stop.

There were four other men in the driver's cab, and the bus remained full, with a few people standing much of the time. It would stop by some tree or rock beside the road, with no village or house visible nearby, and passengers would get on or off. Above the window to the driver's cab was a picture of a smart American-style wooden house, with red maple leaves and waterfalls behind it. Across the top, in capital letters, was the message 'IN ANY HOME IS GOD'. On either side were metallic icons of Hindu gods. The little boy and the conductor wanted their photos taken and laughed a lot at the result.

Approaching Jaisalmer there were modern red and white striped windmills beside the road. Some were already operating and feeding the Rajasthani grid, others were still under construction, and some huge tubular sections lay waiting to be erected. From the ramparts of Jaisalmer fort on top of its rocky outcrop, I looked out across the flat expanse of the desert to see forests of wind farms on the sand-hazy horizon.

It was impossible to imagine this great expanse of desert under water, but that is what the proprietor of a restaurant on the ramparts described to us. He told us that, when the great rains struck the region several years before, he had looked out over an enormous lake stretching as far as the eye could see. The rain had been so heavy that the hard-baked earth could not absorb it, and it was three days before the water soaked away.

* * *

While we filled in the necessary police forms at the hotel, the owner embarrassed us by telling us that we were very noble. He was impressed that Europeans would come to this out-of-the-way corner and give their time and effort to help in the village schools. He and his younger brother owned this eighteenth century *haveli*, where we ate supper on the roof, with the floodlit fort towering above us.

"One of our ancestors worked as an architect for the Maharaja," he told us, "and the Maharaja gave him this house as a reward for his services."

He explained that his family was Brahmin, and because of the government's reverse discrimination laws they had found it hard to get work, so they had turned the *haveli* into a hotel. (These reverse discrimination laws reserve places in educational establishments and jobs in government services for people from the lower castes.) Lena and I shared a beautiful clean room, with cushioned window seats in front of tall, elegant, shuttered windows, looking out on a quiet narrow street.

We were hungry, and Lena's guidebook recommended the Trio restaurant, inside the fort. After wandering through the bazaar, skirting round cows and occasionally bulls, we found the restaurant in a large open square, or *chowk*. A big bull with magnificent long curved horns stood in the middle of the traffic nearby. It amazed me that the bulls there roamed freely and seemed as calm and docile as the cows.

The other customers in the smart rooftop restaurant were mainly Indian families out for a weekend lunch. One group must have been on a visit home from the UK, as they were speaking English and their children had English accents. The food was a welcome change from the cauliflower, pea, carrot and potato curries we usually ate in camp. We were served aubergine and mushroom dishes, and naan bread instead of chapatis.

I loved to wander through the bazaar, looking at the bright bedspreads and hangings displayed on a wall here, and trying to identify the seeds and spices set out in front of a shop there. On one display of bedclothes a notice advertised 'Magic bedsheets – no need for viagra'. I watched a *sadhu* going from shop to shop begging. He was a wild looking man with a bronze begging bowl, wearing a rough saffron garment which left one shoulder bare, and his black hair was long and unkempt. One shopkeeper gave him money in exchange for a blessing, and then consulted him briefly, presumably about some more specific need, for which he received another blessing.

Men squatted at the open doors of their clothes shops and tried to entice us in to see their wares. When we smiled and walked on they would call after us:

"Come to my shop tomorrow."

When I showed an interest in a display of *kurtas*, the owner ushered me in and turned out his wares onto the carpet in front of me. The shopkeepers would always spend a long time chatting with us. Some brought us *chai*, and many of them, when they heard we were from Shiv, would ask if we were teachers, and would remember other volunteers they had met. Each time we visited Jaisalmer these men would recognise us from previous visits, ask after volunteers who were not with us, and offer us *chai*, so our progress through the streets was slow.

We walked into a large, modern Kashmiri shop. Unlike most of the others it had big windows and a front door. The owner welcomed us and closed the door while he gave us a tutorial on pashminas and how to tell the difference between a true pashmina, a Kashmir wool shawl, and shawls made from synthetic fibre. He unlocked a safe and showed us his most precious pashmina – as light as a cobweb but very warm. True pashminas are made only from the hair in the beard of a Kashmir goat. Kashmir shawls are made from hair from other parts of the goat and are a bit heavier and thicker but still very warm. Man-made fibre shawls are thicker and heavier still but not nearly so warm, and they are usually coloured with chemical rather than natural dyes. He showed us how to distinguish them from those made of hair or wool by setting light to a little strand cut from the fringe – the smell of burnt hair identifies natural hair or wool, whereas man-made fibres smell like burnt plastic and melt to a hard little ball. Pure silk does not burn at all.

He told his assistant to bring us *chai*, and when we admired the carpets hanging on the walls he spread some of them out on the floor and told us all about them. He knew our funds were limited and we were not going to buy any carpets, but he seemed to enjoy educating us.

"My family is still living in Kashmir," he said. "I return to my village every year from the middle of March to the end of July. It is very hot in Rajasthan then."

He explained that his family had moved away from the disputed border with Pakistan and were now living just outside Srinigar.

"But they cannot move further away because of their goats. The carpets and pashminas are handmade by people in my village. As soon as I sell one of the carpets I phone home and ask the villagers to start on another one, of exactly the same design, to replace it. Each carpet takes months to make."

* * *

The tale of the girl who was the first bride in her village for a hundred years was not the only story I heard in Jaisalmer that illustrated the problems faced by women in traditional society. There was a handicraft shop near the gate of the fort which had been started to help support child widows. These were women from a particular village who had been child brides, married perhaps as young as four years old to boys from another village. A child bride does not leave her family to live in her husband's home until she reaches puberty. But in this case all the boys died before their brides were old enough to join them. Was there an epidemic in their village? I never found out.

The life of a widow in traditional Indian society had little to recommend it. She could never marry again, and had to discard her jewels and fine saris and spend the rest of her life wearing unadorned white clothing and relying on her relations for the necessities of life.

So the child brides became child widows and could never marry, even though they had never lived with their husbands' families. They were left destitute. Their own families could not afford to keep and feed them for the rest of their lives. So, to help provide them with the necessities of life, the shop sold things they made. I contributed a little by buying two beautiful patchwork bedspreads made from old wedding saris, decorated with little beads and sequins. They were in bright cobalt blue that I was told was the colour of Krishna and was once used for Brahmin wedding dresses.

The year before, just inside the entrance to one of the great forts we visited, I had seen an array of panels on the wall. Each bore the impression of a raised hand and an inscription. They commemorated women who had committed *sati*, the practice of a widow immolating herself on her husband's funeral pyre. Though some may have been coerced into this act, others did it of their own free will. Perhaps, for some, it was better than the life of a widow.

The British government made *sati* illegal in the time of the Raj, but it is difficult to eliminate practices which have been traditional for thousands of years in a country as large, and with such a huge rural population, as India. As late as 1987 the Indian government passed yet another act for the prevention of *sati*.

On one occasion Lena, Bengt and I stayed in a hotel in the fort itself, and from the balcony of my room I could watch the sun set as I looked out to my right, and see it rise again the next morning to my left. We sat with the manager, in the pleasant courtyard planted with bushes and shady trees, while he told us his story.

"I come from Gadra," he said. "Do you know it? It is close to the Pakistani border."

In Shiv I had seen a signpost pointing across the desert to Gadra, eighty kilometres away. Just the other side of the border, inside Pakistan, is a town called Gadra. His family had left it, in the company of other Hindu families, when India and Pakistan were partitioned, and they had crossed the new border into India. There they had built themselves a village and called it Gadra, after the home town to which they could never return.

"There are Hindus left in Pakistani Gadra who would like to move to India, but without passports it is not possible," he told us. "Life in Indian Gadra is hard. I had to start work when I was nine years old, so I had little education."

But he learnt English from talking to tourists in Jaisalmer and had risen to be the manager of this hotel. Now he brought people from his village to work in the kitchens.

"Jaisalmer people are rich," he said, "and do not want to do such work."

While we were talking, a large cow ambled up the street and stopped just outside the entrance to the hotel. I thought she might come into the courtyard, as the door was quite wide enough, but she just stood there until the manager fetched a chapati and gave it to her. She munched it, and when it was gone she moved slowly on.

"She comes at six o'clock every morning and seven every evening, and I always give her a chapati," he said.

She belonged to people in the next street, but toured the neighbourhood every day and was given a chapati here and a handful of grass there because it is good luck to feed a cow.

Another good luck object was a string of seven green chillis with half a lemon and a lump of charcoal below them, which hung at the hotel entrance. We had seen a man going round and hanging such strings at the front of businesses in Shiv the previous morning. He took down the old string, threw it on the ground, and recited prayers as he hung up the new one.

The hotel manager explained:

"These strings are changed every Saturday, and it is good luck if you happen to tread on one of the lemons. There is one chilli on the string for each day of the week, and if the chillis go red during the week it is a sign of bad luck. The kohl at the bottom of the string wards off the evil eye."

In a little souvenir shop the owner was another native of Gadra, and it was he who told me that I was not 'retired' but 're-tyred'.

"Though the body ages, the soul remains young," he said, "and eventually it will be given a new young body."

His words made me feel that a belief in rebirth could be comforting, though Hindus aspire to escape from the endless cycle of death and rebirth and achieve *Moksha* (or Nirvana).

The shopkeeper explained the Indian respect for teachers, saying that you respect first of all your parents, then the gods, and then your teacher.

"The gods," he said, "are always there, but your parents have brought you into the world and so they come first. You cannot live well without the education your teacher gives you, and so the teacher comes next after the gods."

As the time for me to leave Shiv drew near, I hunted in Jaisalmer for little farewell presents to give the children I taught. My eye was caught by key rings decorated with beads, on a tiny stall. When I told the young stallholder I needed a dozen identical key rings for the girls in my class, he said:

"Oh – you are a teacher! I am a student. I'm learning Italian, and I have great respect for teachers."

So he offered them to me at two-thirds his original price.

He had to take us to his storehouse to find enough for my needs and told us that next week it was to be opened as a proper shop. While he hunted through boxes, Bengt found a sandalwood Buddha on a shelf, which he bought after some bargaining, and was asked for one extra rupee for luck because it was the first thing to be bought from this shop. As we left, the young man presented me with another decorated key ring as a gift for myself.

* * *

Barmer was a complete contrast to Jaisalmer. Jaisalmer town is dominated by the ochre fort atop its rocky outcrop, which gives it a historic and romantic look. There was no such landmark in Barmer, and its buildings seemed utilitarian and grey. But it was a bustling town, with the railway station marking its importance as the administrative centre of the district. It was a completely Indian town, and Lena and I saw no other Westerners when we spent a day there.

The road into the centre from the bus terminus was lined with little stalls, and as usual the beautiful displays of vegetables and fruit looked clean and fresh. We came across a procession of women dressed in elegant saris, many of whom had pots with coconut leaves on their heads. Coconut leaves are a sign of marriage, so perhaps it was a wedding procession.

Just up the road from the train station there was a modern-looking shopping centre. Security guards at the entrance were presumably there to keep out anyone too poor to afford the luxuries inside. The ground floor contained a big supermarket and a vegetable and fruit store, as well as shops selling all sorts of sweets, drinks and street food. Upstairs were rows of tables on which were arrayed clothes and shoes, kitchen and household wares, jewellery, cosmetics, and rather flashy pictures and statuettes of the gods. Lena was drawn to the display of shiny metal *tiffin* carriers – cylindrical stacks of two or three dishes which clipped together and had a handle to carry them by. Indians take their lunches to work in these, as we would take a packed lunch in a plastic box.

From a stall on the way back to the bus station I bought thirty-one pages of stickers, as farewell presents for the children at school. They loved little stickers showing 'happy faces' or stars and would use them to decorate their school bags and books. Here I found some showing butterflies and flowers. The woman stallholder spoke no English, but was so delighted with such a big transaction (310 rupees – just under five euro!) that she shook hands enthusiastically several times with Lena as well as me.

* * *

A new group of Danish volunteers had arrived, and two of them replaced Joya and Alex at my school. They were full of enthusiasm and suggested that we should get the children to brush their teeth every day. The children had beautifully white teeth, but they did not own toothbrushes, and many had dark reddish brown marks close to the gum. I discovered later that this was caused by the local water supply, which has a very high fluoride content because of the nature of the rocks in the region.

We bought toothbrushes and toothpaste in Shiv, and the tailor's wife sewed little pockets onto a strip of material so that the children could keep their toothbrushes in their own, individually labelled, pockets. At the end of break every day the children queued up to have toothpaste squeezed onto their brushes, and they loved scrubbing their teeth, sneaking back to try to get a second helping of toothpaste. Then Gopal, the senior boy, would ladle out water into their hands from a metal pot on a stand on the veranda, so that they could rinse their mouths.

Kailash, the teacher, had spoken very little English at first but gradually became more confident of his linguistic ability, and one day, when the bus was late arriving to fetch us back for lunch, I had a long chat with him. He was a dedicated and excellent teacher.

"I am thirty," he told me. "I trained in Barmer, and I have been teaching for eight years. My wife is twenty-eight, and we have a child of six."

Information about the family is always very important, and conversations often start with enquiries about one's parents, siblings and children. Kailash lived in another small village near Shiv and had two brothers living nearby. One was also a teacher and the other owned a shop in Shiv. A third brother was in the army and lived in Delhi.

Every day, after we went back to camp, Kailash fed the children lunch. The Indian government provides funding for a free midday meal for all children attending government schools. Often a proportion of the money disappears into the pockets of local officials and teachers, but Kailash made sure that the children were properly fed and also brought them fruit – bananas or oranges – to eat at break once a week.

* * *

Brightly coloured powders – scarlet, yellow, green and purple – were piled high on dishes on the market stalls in Jaisalmer as the spring festival of Holi drew near. Holi usually falls in March, though like most Hindu festivals the actual date varies, since it is determined by the moon. There are two days of religious rites, before the festival culminates with crowds of people in festive mood throwing coloured powder at one another in the streets. In Jaisalmer the local Brahmins collect money and organise a huge feast on the night of the second day. Thousands of people gather to eat and drink beside a lake where sacred carp swim, next to a little temple.

We celebrated, rather demurely, in camp. First Rinku and her older sister (who had joined Rinku working in the kitchen) came out with colours on a tray and painted pink and green stripes on my face and Lena's, and we reciprocated by smearing them with colour. Later the executives who were left in camp – tall Vishal, Sanjay and Arpet – appeared, with their faces and clothes streaked all over with red, green and purple, looking a bit like Red Indians in warpaint. The Danish girls had bought some coloured powders, and the proceedings became wilder. We were all streaked with colour and sprayed with water. But at midday the colour throwing traditionally ends, and we went to change and wash before lunch.

Hindus love celebrations and festivals. On the religious feast of *Shivratri* – literally the night of Shiva – school was closed for the day. One week was particularly propitious for weddings, and music and drumming could be heard far into the night from the village, where marriages were being celebrated with big parties. Our afternoon class in Shiv was cancelled because the tailor and his wife had relations visiting for a family wedding.

Then one afternoon Lena and I met Ashvini, Sanjay and tall Vishal coming back from Shiv where they had been buying ingredients for a celebratory rice pudding for Ashvini's twenty-second birthday. They invited us to join the party, so we changed into our best *salwar kameez* and brought along little presents for Ashvini – balloons decorated with the Swedish flag, a pack of cards, and the little keyring I had been given in Jaisalmer. It was a quiet party, with only four or five of the staff, Lena and myself. We feasted on rice pudding, cooked with sultanas and cashew nuts.

Tall Vishal announced that he would also celebrate his birthday before Lena and I left and would invite us to the party. Ashvini's birthday pudding had been cooked rather quickly because the others had only discovered it was his birthday that afternoon.

"A real birthday rice pudding needs long, slow cooking. You shall taste one," Vishal said.

In fact his birthday was not until the autumn, but he provided a slowly cooked rice pudding for an early celebration just before the time came for us to leave.

The new camp manager, Vishal-ji (to distinguish him from tall Vishal), arranged a big party for all the volunteers and executives on our last evening. It started with musical chairs in the dining hall, followed by a table quiz, with forfeits for the two losing teams. Then the camp lights were turned off for a treasure hunt round the grounds with torches. In the dark we stumbled over stones and pricked our toes on spiky thistle-like plants. We were looking for pieces of paper, each with a letter on, which would spell a word when we had finally collected them all. My team soon realised that the word was 'Goodbye', but we failed to find the final 'e' which had been placed with a lot of paper rubbish in an old unused brick stove.

* * *

The desert fascinated me. I still visit it in my dreams – the vast flat expanse of stony sand, dotted with small shrubby acacia, where the wind whips up dust devils. Overhead is the huge blue sky, shading through paler blue to a hazy fawn where sand hangs in the air near the horizon. Perhaps it is the sand in the air which creates the dramatic sunsets. The light becomes opalescent as the sun sinks like a deep crimson ball to the horizon. After that it becomes dark very quickly.

At night the sky is clear and black. The stars are brilliant. The Milky Way is like an arch above me, and high in the sky to the south is Orion the hunter, with the bright dog star Sirius below at his heels, while Taurus the bull faces him. Mars, glowing a bloody red, is quite high in the south-east. It rises higher in the sky every night. Earlier there was a planet setting in the west as darkness fell – Venus, perhaps, though it too looked red because of the sand in the air near the horizon.

There are so many things I miss – the bulbuls with their bubbly song in the tree behind the dining hall in the mornings; the 'oo took took oo roo' of the little brown doves – three syllables longer than the 'coo coo' of the collared doves; the black goats standing on their hind legs to eat leaves from the henna bushes; the humped cows; camel carts and ox carts on the road; the hot sun and blue sky; the friends I made. But above all I miss the children, at the village school and at the afternoon class in Shiv.

As we walked to the English and Computing class, Merra joined us in the street and took my hand. She said:

"Is tomorrow your last day?"

"Yes. I'm leaving Shiv at the weekend."

"I am sad."

When Hitesh and I went along to the tailor's house the following afternoon the girls were not there yet. Apparently they were finishing off their goodbye cards for me. The tailor's daughter arrived home and was hungry. So her mother went across the street to a vendor's cart and brought back something for Hitesh and myself as well – a tray of little fried pastry balls. You had to break a hole in one with a finger and insert some sticky spicy concoction which was then topped up with a sour liquid. You then had to put the whole thing in your mouth in one go. I enjoyed them, but I found them difficult to eat without getting juice on my chin.

When the girls arrived they gave me lovely cards, homemade on pink paper (which we had provided for them to write on in the class earlier in the week because there was no white paper left in camp). The cards were all decorated with pictures of flowers and hearts, and said that I was their best friend and best teacher, they would miss me, and they were sad. Merra tied a little silvery bracelet on my wrist (which she had made herself), and Varsha gave me a pair of dangly silvery earrings. I gave the girls the presents I had bought for them – the little beaded key rings from Jaisalmer, decorative *bindis* from the tailor's shop and some fruit sweets. Then it was goodbye time. I hugged each one of the girls, and the tailor's wife shook hands very warmly and put a spot of pink powder on my cheek for good luck.

* * *

My last morning at the village school was a memorable and emotional occasion. I was the only volunteer there that day because the Danish girls had taken a week off to do some sightseeing. After toothbrushing we had one game of 'days of the week', and then Kailash arranged the whole school sitting in rows in front of my blackboard. He explained to them that I was going home, and told them:

"Sara-ji has said that she would like to come back to India again, and so you should pray to the God that she comes back to us next year."

Sangita came up to me and put a garland round my neck. She was followed by Lali, who placed a red mark on my forehead, dipping her finger in the bag of red powder that Kailash held out. Then each of my class in turn came up and, dipping their fingers in the powder, smeared my cheeks, my arms and my clothes with red. Last of all Gopal came up and put a *ladoo* in my mouth. *Ladoos* were passed round, and everyone took a piece.

I gave the children the stickers I had bought for them, as

well as some brightly coloured pens and sticky date and nut confectionery. I gave Kailash the inflatable globe and the atlas I had brought from home, which I was leaving for the school. He presented me with a plastic music box – a typically gaudy Indian affair which played a Rajasthani folk song at the press of a button. As it played, the central section rotated, decorated with coloured flowers surrounding a pink rose and 'LOVE' written in big mauve letters. He had inscribed on it 'from Kailash, HM, Govt School'. By this point I was almost in tears, but then it was time for photographs. Ashvini, using my camera, took a photo of me with each child in the school in turn and finally with Kailash. And then the minibus arrived, and Kailash lined up all the children beside it to wave goodbye.

Everyone on the bus wondered why I was still celebrating Holi, and when Hitesh got on he exclaimed:

"Oh, Sara, what has happened to you?"

When I explained he told me:

"They have honoured you. This ceremony has religious significance. I have seen it performed so often for pilgrims returning home."

* * *

I may not have been on a pilgrimage, but the seven weeks at Shiv had given me a new perspective. I found the department stores at home depressing, with a plethora of goods, most of which seemed to me unnecessary and extravagant. The products on cosmetic counters all claimed to be 'new' and 'improved', as though everyone were locked in an upward spiral, always searching for change for the sake of change. Dress shops were crammed with clothes which would be discarded and replaced as soon as they went out of fashion.

Advertisements everywhere urged me to buy things I did not need – a particular brand of beer, the latest mobile phone, a new television set, a new sofa. Everything must be new – if something breaks it cannot be repaired, it must be replaced. Europeans are horrified at the rubbish strewn around in India, but so much of what we throw away here would be recycled there – poor families scavenge on heaps of refuse for plastic bottles, rags, scraps of metal and anything else that can be re-used and that will earn them a few rupees. And the Indians are adept at repairing machinery. When I visited Darjeeling several years later, the chief engineer explained to me proudly how he repaired and maintained the ancient steam engines which still drew trains of tourists on the hill railway.

I had always thought most of the commercials on television ridiculous. Now I no longer even found them amusing. Their claims to have the best interests of the public at heart were so clearly false. Slogans such a 'You're worth it', 'Every little helps', or 'We're in it (brewing) for the love of it' mean nothing. Their intent is simply to boost the advertiser's own profits.

I became very aware of the way that money dominates everything. The news that Rory McIlroy had won another golf tournament was always immediately followed by the enormous amount of prize money involved. Participants in quiz shows on television do not enter for fun, but in the expectation of winning huge prizes. In televised cookery competitions people vie for big financial rewards. In one, aspiring chefs were provided with a random selection of ingredients with which they had to improvise a dish within the short timeframe of the TV programme. I found this particularly distasteful, because they were just playing with food. In Shiv, food is a basic necessity, which some find hard to afford, and which nobody takes for granted or wastes.

The Irish agency who organised my volunteering placement told me that I was suffering from reverse culture shock. But this disillusion with the consumer society does not go away, and I have spoken to other returned volunteers whose outlook has been changed in a similar way.

Chapter 4

GODS AND MEN NORTH AND SOUTH

On the slope of the desolate river among tall grasses I asked her,

"Maiden, where do you go shading your lamp with your mantle?

My house is all dark and lonesome – lend me your light."

She raised her dark eyes for a moment and looked at my face through the dusk.

"I have come to the river", she said, "to float my lamp on the stream when the daylight wanes in the west."

As we drifted on the river in the fading light, this verse by Rabindranath Tagore came to my mind. The pretty girl in the bows lit four lamps, little candles each in its bowl of flowers, and handed two each to Brian and me.

"Float one of them in the river," Krishna, our guide, told us.

When we had set them sailing on the dark waters he took the other two from us and said prayers as he floated one on either side of the boat. The little lights bobbed out to join others, and the river was spangled with flickering stars.

Here only the far, eastern shore of the river, the holy Ganges, is desolate and barren. On the western bank ancient buildings rise from the *ghats* at the water's edge. Varanasi, once called Benares, in the northern state of Uttar Pradesh, is a holy city. Pilgrims bathe ritually from the *ghats*, drink the holy water, and process through the streets near the water's edge chanting, beating drums and playing musical instruments.

We joined the pilgrims at the evening prayers to the river, Mother Ganga. Seven priests, in gorgeous robes of cream and pink, stood on seven platforms above the river, blowing conches and weaving patterns in the air with sticks of incense. The pilgrims listened silently as the priests chanted and bells were rung. The mothball smell of camphor drifted over us as lamps were lit to accompany prayers to Shiva, for Varanasi is a place where the god burst into the sky as a pillar of light. Some pilgrims with shaved heads had sacrificed their hair. They all sat cross-legged, rapt and immobile.

The river is lined with temples, palaces built by visiting rajas, hostels for pilgrims, and homes for widows. To die in Varanasi liberates the soul from the endless cycle of death and rebirth. At the funeral *ghats*, flames flicker as bodies, shrouded in white, are cremated. The ashes are consigned to the river. If a Hindu cannot be cremated at Varanasi, the next best thing is to have his ashes scattered there. On the flight out I had met a young Indian with a strong Manchester accent. He was visiting India for the first time in his life, taking his mother's ashes to the Ganges at Varanasi.

* * *

Brian and I were in Varanasi thanks to Amitabh, our guide from the year before. He had organised a tour for us, eastward from Delhi to Uttar and Madhya Pradesh, and Brian had flown out to join me when I left Shiv. We were provided with a car and driver, and our own local guide in every place we visited.

The following year Amitabh arranged a trip for us to tropical Tamil Nadu and Kerala in the far south. The languages spoken in the southern states are completely different from the Indo-European languages of the north and are written in curvaceous scripts nothing like Devanagari. So my smattering of Hindi was of no use to me there.

In Tamil Nadu we followed the famous Hindu temple trail, before driving across the hills of the Western Ghats to Kerala – a land of spices and paddy fields, where I saw pelicans and breadfruit trees.

"These young people are Dravidians," Krishna had explained, referring to the girl with the lamps and her brothers who rowed our boat on the Ganges at Varanasi. "They are students here and have come from the south."

"The Dravidians moved southwards as Aryan invaders moved in from the north," one of my Rajasthani colleagues told me. "They are darker skinned than us, less warlike and more artistic."

But I did not find the people I met on our trip to the far south markedly different from the northerners. Some were certainly darker, but the strong tropical sun there can darken already brown skin. Brian and I found the same friendliness and interest in the people we met, and our driver was a delightful young man who became a friend during the two weeks we spent with him.

New analysis[3] has shown that there are two main genetic types in India. In the very distant past one was associated with the north and the other with the south of the subcontinent. However, modern Indians from all over the country show a mixture of these types, and this mixing of genes occurred over an interval of about two thousand years, starting around the time of the Aryan invasion roughly four thousand years ago. That this mixing stopped two thousand years later is attributed to the introduction of strict caste marriage laws. But whether or not there really are deep racial

3 *The American Journal of Human Genetics*, Volume 93, Issue 3, 5 September 2013, pp 422-438.

differences between those from the north and the south, Hinduism transcends them and unites people across the whole vast country.

One evening we stood outside the great gate of the temple at Madurai. Just inside we could see Nandi, the white bull of Shiva, waiting to lead the procession. Pilgrims thronged the street. Some were groups of young men with grave looks on their faces, their black hair and black clothing giving them an intimidating appearance. But when they saw us, one group broke into broad smiles and came up to shake our hands, while another group posed to be photographed.

Pilgrims had been flocking to the temple all day.

"That group are from Gujarat, and the next from Rajasthan," said our guide.

"How can you tell?" I asked.

"Oh, by the style and colour of their clothing."

These pilgrims had travelled thousands of kilometres from the north to attend this festival in the far south-eastern state of Tamil Nadu.

It was completely dark by the time there was movement from inside the temple, and the white bull appeared, his humped back covered in a magnificently embroidered scarlet cloth. He was led by a man beating a small drum, and followed by two beautifully caparisoned camels. Then came the temple elephant, her face painted with white spots and patterns and her back covered with another brightly patterned cloth. After a short pause the figure of Ganesh in an ornate wooden shrine appeared, set on a wheeled cart pushed by four men. Finally a group of men heaved out a trolley carrying a huge carved wooden shrine. Its massive weight made it difficult for them to make the turn onto the road. Inside it, brightly illuminated, were the figures of Shiva and his consort Parvati.

* * *

The great gods, Brahma, Vishnu and Shiva, and the elephant-headed God of Good Fortune, Ganesh, are recognised and worshipped throughout the country. But other deities may be local, or given different names in the north and the south.

"There are ten incarnations of Vishnu," our guide explained as we stood in front of ten carved pillars, each bearing a representation of one of the incarnations. "Rama is the seventh incarnation. In the north the Buddha is identified as the ninth incarnation, immediately following Krishna. But in the south the Buddha is not recognised as an incarnation, and here you see an eighth deity between Rama and Krishna. That incarnation is not accepted in the north."

The first of the ten carvings showed a fish, and the second a turtle.

"Successive incarnations follow the path of evolution, from fish upwards, through primitive man, until they reach Rama, who is a modern man," said our guide. "The tenth incarnation is yet to come. It has the head of a horse." He laughed. "Perhaps it is an alien!"

Hinduism is not so rigid a system that it cannot accept local differences in belief and practice.

"Buddhism and Jainism are really just different forms of Hinduism," one guide told us, though I suspect the practitioners of either of these religions would have disagreed with him.

At one time or another over the millennia the gods of different communities have been absorbed and re-interpreted within the Hindu pantheon. But Hinduism also embraces the concept of one supreme deity. Brahman is the primal essence, without beginning or end, the ultimate unifying principle of the universe. Brahma, Vishnu, Shiva and all the other gods are different manifestations of this impersonal and spiritual source of all existence. In a religious column in the *Times of India* I read an article by a Hindu theologian who wrote that it does not matter what one calls the god to whom one prays. All who pray are addressing the same God.

* * *

Islam and Christianity remain completely separate religions. Their insistence on the rejection of other beliefs makes it impossible to absorb them into Hinduism. However, one middle-aged man in Rajasthan told me that his daughter was a Christian minister. When I asked if he himself was Christian he replied:

"I believe in Jesus Christ and the New Testament," and I suspected that he had simply added the Christian God to the Hindu deities he revered.

Muslims still make up over fourteen per cent of the population of India, the largest religious group after the Hindus (eighty per cent). Christians come next at just over two per cent. The percentage of the population that is Sikh, Buddhist or Jain is smaller still.

It is not always easy for a visitor to identify a member of one of these groups. They observe the rites of their own religions, but apart from that their lifestyles are very similar to those of their Hindu neighbours. It was only several years later, when I saw the film *Tana Bana*[4], that I realised the silk weavers I had seen in Varanasi were Muslim.

Education is not segregated by religion (apart from the Muslim madrasas). Many non-Christian children attend Catholic schools, or schools originally set up by Protestant missionaries, because of their good educational standards. An education at one of the many 'English medium' schools, which teach through English, is prized. A good knowledge of English is seen as providing access to better jobs.

Tensions between Muslims and Hindus flare up every so often, with terrible bloodshed. In Varanasi on a Friday I asked why armed soldiers were on the street.

---

4 Tana Bana is produced by *Underground Films & Mudita Productions* and funded by the *Simon Cumbers Media Fund* in association with the *Irish Film Board.*

"You are close to a mosque, and the soldiers are here to make sure there is no trouble," was the reply.

But people of different faiths can also make good neighbours. I visited an ancient Jewish synagogue in the south, where the orthodox Jewish population was very elderly. There were no longer enough men to make the quorum of ten needed for the prayer service. None of the younger generation lived nearby. However, the local people, whether they were Hindu, Muslim or Christian, looked after their elderly Jewish neighbours, doing their shopping when they were unable to do it themselves and checking on them to see if they needed any sort of help.

In India, official state holidays are celebrated not only on Hindu feast days but on Muslim and Christian ones as well. Christmas and Eid rank alongside Divali and Holi.

In my third year of volunteering I lived for four weeks with a Christian family in Jaipur. They lived a life very similar to other middle-class Indians. In a Christmas email my host wrote:

"My daughter-in-law has been baking Christmas cakes. We have to have one when we entertain our Hindu neighbours because they like it very much."

One weekend when I was in Kolkata my Hindu guide took me to a covered market and pointed out a shop which had been owned by Jews for several generations.

"That is the only place in the city where we can buy hot cross buns and Christmas cake," she said. "My friends and I always go there to buy them around Easter and Christmas times."

* * *

There is a large number of Christians in the south, in particular in Kerala, where they make up nineteen per cent of the population. This is not only the result of European evangelisation. There is documentary evidence from the fourth century of a community of Christians in the south associated with the Syrian Orthodox Church. Their traditions go back to Saint Thomas, but they became part of the Syrian Orthodox Church, under the Patriarch of Antioch, in the third or fourth century. Aramaic is still used in their services.

Legend has it that Saint Thomas the apostle travelled to southern India in the middle of the first century AD, long before Christianity reached northern Europe. The cathedral in Chennai is dedicated to him. The crucifix behind the altar depicts Christ on the cross rising, crowned and robed, from a lotus, flanked by peacocks. In Pondicherry the Virgin is depicted wearing an elegant sari.

In the north, the small communities of Christians were converted more recently by European missionaries. The great grandparents of my host in Jaipur had been converted by Scottish missionaries in the mid nineteenth century. He told me:

"The missionaries came and provided things the people needed – schools and medical care. And they brought famine relief after several disastrous droughts."

Since 1970 the different Protestant denominations in northern India have been united under the Church of North India. It combines many traditions and makes allowance for a diversity of religious interpretations and practices. Similarly, in the south, the different Protestant churches were united as the Church of South India at Independence in 1947.

* * *

Traditional Hindu temple architecture is very different in the north and south of the country. In the north I admired the beauty of the ancient temples of Khajuraho, set in grassy parkland bright with flowering flame trees and bougainvillea. They are built of ochre sandstone and each is intricately carved with gods and men, dancers and musicians, camels, horses and elephants, and the erotic scenes for which the site is famous. The four main spires of each temple rise like steps from lowest to highest.

"They are like a mountain range and represent the four stages of life," our guide told us. "The lowest represents birth and childhood, the next working life, the third married life, and the highest is release from worldly desires. Not everyone reaches this last, ascetic, state."

In contrast, I found the southern temples that I saw in Tamil Nadu rather garish. They have single spires, decorated with stucco figures of gods and men painted in bright blues, reds and yellows. A temple elephant stands inside the outer gate, dispensing blessings in return for a coin which she takes with her trunk and passes to her mahout. A ten rupee note is the price for a tourist. She gently rested her trunk on my head, and I felt her warm, hay scented breath on my forehead.

It is from the south that the beautiful bronzes come, depicting Shiva, with flowing hair, dancing the world into being within a circle of flame. It almost seems that, in the south, he has usurped the roles of Brahma, the creator, and Vishnu, the preserver.

The festivals are different too. We were in the south during the nine-day feast of Pongal, at the time of the first rice harvest of the year. Houses were decorated with sheaves of sugar cane, and we were served a special rice dish. Cattle had their horns painted in red, yellow or green, ready for their procession, harnessed with brightly coloured ropes, to the temple on the final day of the feast.

In the north, Pongal is not celebrated, but a festival for the wheat harvest, dedicated to Durga, coincided with our visit to Khajuraho. In a tiny dark shrine, where even I had to stoop to enter, little bowls containing green shoots of wheat were spread in front of the goddess. They would be consigned to the waters of the local lake at the culmination of the festival.

Holi, which welcomes the spring, is a northern festival for a northern season. In the tropical south there is no spring in the sense of an annual rebirth of plants and animals after winter. But through modern communications and television, people in the south can see the excitement and fun of the colour festival, and the celebration of Holi has become popular throughout India.

* * *

In southern India, at the foot of stairs rising to a temple to Ganesh perched on top of a rocky tor, I came across a tree hung with coloured rags.

"Each rag is the prayer of a woman longing for a child," the holy man sitting beside the tree told me.

In Ireland such trees, representing the same hopes and prayers, can sometimes still be found in the countryside. We call them 'fairy trees'. Could these trees in India and Ireland hark back to some much earlier religion, dating from a time ages before the Aryan invasion of India, or even before humans spread out south-east into India and north-west into Europe?

The Aryan incursion occurred almost two thousand years before the birth of Christ. They brought with them the Sanskrit language and the Vedas, the ancient Hindu holy books. But their religion has its origins in a much earlier past. Indra, King of the Gods in the Rigveda (the oldest of the Vedas), is similar to Thor, Zeus and other early European gods. He is a thunder god, carrying a hammer, and is associated with Agni, a god of fire.

Indra is said to have led cattle raids, which immediately made me think of the Irish epic, the *Táin Bó Cúailnge* – the *Cattle Raid of Cooley*. The stories in the *Mahabharata*, of the wars and rivalries between two great clans, painted a picture for me of a civilisation similar to that depicted in the Irish legends of the wars in which the great hero Cú Chulainn fought.

In Christian Europe these tales have been relegated to the realms of mythology and almost forgotten. In contrast, in India they have been preserved as early documents concerning the Hindu religion. Hinduism evolves – Brahma, Vishnu and Shiva have eclipsed Indra, but he has not been eradicated, merely demoted to the position of a minor god. Perhaps this inclusive rather than exclusive development is what has preserved Hinduism as the oldest of the world's great living religions.

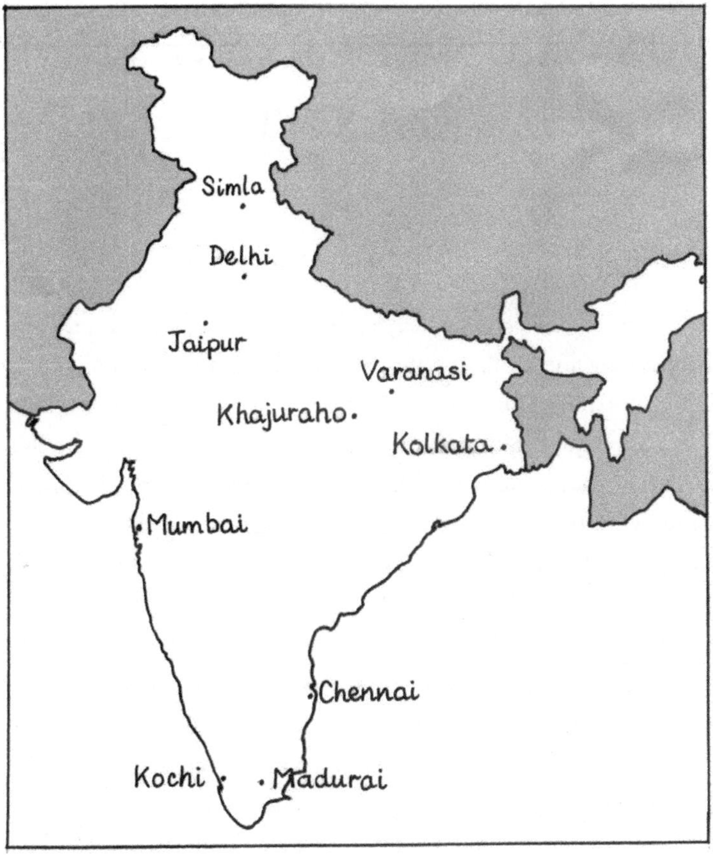

Map of India

Chapter 5

VOLUNTEERING IN LALSOT

My time in Shiv had increased my fascination with India, and I found teaching young children interesting and fulfilling. I was determined to go back as a volunteer the following year. But after I left Shiv, the three-year drought in the Thar desert was broken by heavy monsoon rains. The mud brick huts of the volunteer camp, with their thatched roofs, were badly damaged. So the Shiv camp was closed, and when I returned to Rajasthan the following January it was to the volunteer organisation's second camp, near Lalsot, about eighty kilometres south-east of Jaipur.

This camp was in farming country, less stark and austere than the desert, but I found it beautiful in other ways. When I arrived the fields were dark green with young wheat or golden yellow with mustard flowers. Later the flowers faded to leave pale green fronds, all bending and swaying together, so that the fields looked like a gently billowing sea. Later still I would see villagers harvesting the fronds with sickles.

As the season progressed, the acid yellow of cumin flowers replaced the warmer yellow of the mustard. Tall elegant golden grasses lined the roadside, and flocks of little birds foraged among them, their wings glowing russet as they flitted from stalk to stalk. A banyan tree beside a village well gave deep shade for the men who sat there talking, its trunk expanded to an enormous girth by the aerial roots which formed a forest of columns all round it. But the hills on the horizon were bare, and where the ground was not cultivated and irrigated it was dry and sandy.

Giri, one of the executives, had studied Indian history and culture at college and was a mine of information about the lives of the people around us.

"The people are happy this year," he told me. "After last summer's heavy monsoon the crop is good, and they will get a high price for their mustard seed."

"What is it used for? Cooking?"

"No, that's not the main use. The oil is a protection against infection. Newborn babies are rubbed with a little of it (only a very little, as it is hot and pungent) and newborn calves have a small amount poured down their throats."

I asked Giri about the rows of white beehives on uncultivated land near the flowering crops.

"They belong to people from West Bengal. They take their hives from place to place, according to the season," he told me. "Later on, when the flowers start to bloom in the Himalayas, they will move there."

They lived in tents in the field with their hives, but I saw no women or children with them. Their families must have stayed in West Bengal with the older generation, while the menfolk travelled.

"They provide honey to big companies that forbid them to sell it locally," Giri said, "but sometimes we can persuade them to sell us a little."

* * *

The itinerant beekeepers were just one of a diversity of groups and castes that I was to discover there. I only saw them as we passed by in the minibus on the way to school but Snake Charmers lived right beside the volunteer camp. A rough track led from the main road to our camp and skirted the edge of the Snake Charmers' village.

It was more an encampment than a village, with a few tiny rectangular brick huts, well spaced over an area of sandy ground. Some were thatched, and sheets of blue plastic, that had protected them from the monsoon rains, were still hanging from the roofs. Others had corrugated iron roofs, held down by rows of stones. Cooking pots were stacked in the outdoor kitchen areas. There were two or three rough shelters in spaces between huts, and a wooden cart stood beside a pile of sacks. A camel and a couple of cows were tethered in the open.

Whenever we walked back to camp we had to run the gauntlet of groups of ragged and (unusually for India) rather dirty children. They would follow us closely, asking, "What is your name?" and wanting to touch our clothes and look at whatever we were carrying.

Once, when another volunteer and I attempted to reach the road by ourselves, the little girls thronged round us, stroking our arms and pulling at our scarves. We could hardly move, and when we had given up and turned back I discovered my watch was missing. I was not unduly worried as it was an old and cheap one, but my companion was very upset to think that these children would steal from us. Usually I found Indian people very honest. On the train, I had been amazed to see two young men plug their mobile phones into the charger (which was provided under every window) and go away for two or three hours. They apparently had no fear that their phones would be stolen.

Kirti was the executive who organised classes for the Snake Charmer children. When I explained to her that my watch had been taken, she went out and spoke to some of the adults. One of the men went round and questioned the children, and returned from a group close to the road, holding out my watch.

"*Dhanyavad*," I said – at least I knew how to say 'thank you' in Hindi – and we parted with polite *namastes*.

The Snake Charmers are members of a Rajasthani tribe called the Kalbelia. Although I had heard of them in Shiv, and one of the volunteers there had taught in a Snake Charmer village, I had never seen that village nor met any of the villagers. They have their own language and were originally a nomadic people. They would have been untouchables before the laws which banned untouchability. They reminded me of Gypsies, and indeed the Gypsies are said to have originated in northern India.

The traditional occupation of the Snake Charmers is to catch snakes, provide cures for snake bites, and to exhibit their cobras at Hindu festivals. In spite of their low caste, they have traditionally been regarded as priests of the snake. They take part in the ritual at Hindu weddings and other religious festivals, for the cobra is sacred to Shiva. Now, of course, they are also a tourist attraction. The snakes I had seen outside Amber Fort in Jaipur moved very languidly when the covers were lifted from their baskets and they heard the music of the pipes. I thought they must be drugged, but Ravi, the executive with me, said:

"No, if they were drugged their dance would be much more lively."

There were only two snakes in the Snake Charmers' village, and one was away taking part in a festival for most of the time I was there. One day a teenage lad approached me as I returned to camp. As he lifted the lid of the basket he was carrying, a cobra reared up towards him.

"If snake bite, I die," he said, clearly wanting to alarm me.

But Ravi told me that the fangs are removed when a cobra is caught.

The Snake Charmer children did not go to school, but Kirti and a couple of volunteers taught them every afternoon, under one of the shelters in the village. They were wild and undisciplined, grubby and unkempt. The volunteers asked for them to be washed before they came to class. Though the adults washed themselves at the pump beside the road, it was a great novelty for the children. One little girl stroked her arms in amazement and delight after her shower and showed off her clean skin to me.

* * *

Every morning I was woken by the '*chup chup*' of a red-wattled lapwing, parading up and down outside the back window of my hut. It sounded like the Hindi for 'quiet quiet', but when I opened the shutters it would leap into the air in a flurry, making a great fuss and noise, and fly round and round with yellow legs trailing out behind. When I opened my door, two little owls would be perched sleepily on the roof of the neighbouring hut. They roosted in the thatch during the day. In the evening they flew screeching around the camp, preparing for a night's hunting. Mynahs strutted about near the dining hall, hopping in to scavenge for crumbs, like overgrown sparrows. In this camp we washed our dishes at a sink inside the hall, with conventional yellow washing-up liquid instead of the blue soap we used at Shiv.

The open space behind the camp and the Snake Charmers' village was common land. Herds of sheep and goats were led across the sparse grass in the mornings and back again in the evenings. One day I saw a large herd of camels grazing there.

"They probably belong to Rebari people," Giri said.

"Who are the Rebari?"

"They are nomadic herders of camels and cattle," he replied. "They move from one piece of common land to another to pasture their animals. The common areas are becoming fewer, but there are still some Rebari living a semi-nomadic life."

One morning on the way to school we encountered a group of these nomads. The minibus was forced to stop, as a herd of cattle streamed towards us on a narrow road, hemmed in by bushy hedgerows on either side. We were engulfed by a jostling throng of well over a hundred animals, with humped backs and curved horns. They were led by an old man in traditional white *dhoti* and *kurta*. Two younger men further back in the midst of the herd urged them on. Bringing up the rear were half a dozen donkeys, laden with packs bulging with blankets, kitchen utensils and bundles of all kinds. Beside them walked a group of women and children, and a young man carrying a baby.

The herds need water as well as pasture. In this area water is not in such short supply as in the Thar desert, but crops like wheat depend on electric power to pump water from below the ground. Cereal crops, such as millet, sorghum and maize, which were traditionally grown in this region, require less irrigation than wheat. But they were not in great demand outside Rajasthan, and so they have been replaced by crops for which there is a larger market and which attract higher prices. However, large-scale irrigation is depleting the water table faster than it can be replenished. The monsoon is not dependable and, with the retreat of glaciers and reduced snowfall in the Himalayas, water will become an increasingly scarce commodity.

Not far from the camp was a large sandy area that I thought must be some kind of quarry. The people digging huge pits in the ground were women in scarlet or orange saris. They were using shovels, and carrying away the earth in great baskets on their heads, to dump it in piles around the edges of their excavation. A few men, in traditional white dress with big white turbans on their heads, seemed to be organising the work. But this was not a quarry.

"Geologists consulted by the government have decided that this is a good place to dig a lake," Giri explained. "It will be a new water supply for the local village."

"Are the villagers doing the digging?"

"No. The government has offered paid work here to people who are very poor, especially women."

One day there was nobody digging there, but all the women were queuing up outside a building, waiting to be paid.

I found an interesting book about Rajasthani folklore and traditions[5] in the library in the recreation hall in camp. It explained that in the past villagers had made and maintained their own wells or ponds. In some places water would seep up through the sand if they dug down far enough. In others they created reservoirs filled by monsoon rains. Every village had a knowledgeable person who could predict the best place to dig. Now the state government has taken over the provision of water, and the villagers no longer provide and maintain ponds for themselves.

Although there was no water problem in the camp, the electricity supply was very unreliable. The power was usually off for much of the day, and if it had not come back on at dusk Vishal, the camp manager, would start a small generator. But it usually came on again later and stayed on all night. I would see the light on the mosquito-repellent jar glowing red if I woke in the dark.

There were far more trees here than around Shiv, and so wood, rather than electricity, was used to heat water in a tall blue cylinder in the open space between the recreation hall and the huts. But the weather was cool for the first few weeks, and the water did not get hot enough for a bucket shower until after breakfast.

* * *

This time I was the only 'grown-up', as the Indians called those in the over thirties groups. A youth group, mainly nineteen- and twenty-year-olds, arrived at the same time that I did. They were

5 *Rajasthan, an oral history: conversations with Komal Kothari*, by Rustom Bharucha, Penguin Books India 2003.

enthusiastic and good company in camp, and I got on well with them, but inevitably my leisure interests often differed from theirs – I was never interested in going to nightclubs in Jaipur at the weekend. However, Thea, from Germany, who was older than most of them, shared my interest in birds, and she joined me on several weekend excursions.

The volunteer camp was similar to the one at Shiv, with rows of little thatched huts arranged in threes round a courtyard. A ten-minute walk down the main road towards Lalsot brought us to a village, with one or two shops and a couple of stalls selling fruit and vegetables. But we had little contact with the people there, and it was smaller and less friendly than Shiv.

Lalsot, twelve kilometres away, was a small town rather than a village. Two main roads met at its centre. One led to Dausa, the nearest town with a railway station, which lies on the great Jaipur-Agra toll road fifty kilometres to the north. The other led out north-westward and provided an alternative route to Jaipur. Both these roads carried a heavy traffic of huge lorries, buses and cars.

One evening a week the minibus drove us in to Lalsot so that we could do some shopping. Off the main road was a maze of little streets lined with tiny open-fronted shops, where it was easy to get lost. I made for the fruit and vegetable market. Its stalls were piled high with tempting fresh-looking produce, though underfoot the narrow unpaved lane was strewn with refuse. Hairy pigs wandered around, and I had to stand to one side when a cow pushed its way between the shoppers. Guavas were in season, and so were oranges – my favourites were the little ones with green patches on the skin. Guavas grew locally, and there was a big guava farm some kilometres up the road beyond our camp.

I already knew Vishal, the camp manager, as he had been manager at Shiv for my last few weeks there. He told me that Kailash, the headmaster at my school in the desert, had phoned several times to ask when the Shiv camp would re-open and provide volunteers again. But there was no prospect of it opening this year.

Ravi, the executive who had collected me from Delhi, came from Himachal Pradesh. Most of the others, including Giri, and Manoj who accompanied me to school, were Rajasthani. In this camp two of the executives were young women, Kirti and Yashoda. Kirti was usually dressed in jeans and a T-shirt, while Yashoda always wore *salwar kameez.* They were both devotees of Parvati, the consort of Shiva, and fasted for one day every week.

Another, slightly older, woman joined the kitchen staff. She was always dressed beautifully in colourful and eye-catching *salwar kameez* and was a friendly and out-going person. One day she told me that her husband had died. But she refused to wear widow's weeds and rely on her relations. Instead she was working here to provide a living for herself and her young son. I got the impression that she was not from a very low caste or a poverty-stricken background, otherwise she might not have had the freedom to choose independence.

A birthday was always an excuse for an evening party. The Indians piled up logs and made a campfire, and we sat round its flickering flames in the dark, drinking Kingfisher beer and feasting on biscuits and chocolate. Vishal brought out a drum, and Shambhu, the cook, sang to its accompaniment. He had a great repertoire of traditional Rajasthani songs which entranced us all.

* * *

On one trip to Lalsot, two of the eighteen-year-old girls were upset by the behaviour of the middle-aged owner of the shop where they usually bought soft drinks, sweets and biscuits. He started to get over-familiar, patting their shoulders and putting an arm round them. At first the girls did not really believe what was happening, and when he offered to take them to see a good film one of them asked:

"Bollywood?"

"No," he said. "Look," and brought out his mobile phone to show them an excerpt.

At that point they realised he was offering them a blue movie. They were horrified, and told Vishal, who was shopping for camp necessities nearby.

Vishal confronted the man, who denied everything. So he went to the police station to file a complaint. The police are notoriously bad at dealing with Indian victims of rape and assault, but apparently they are keen to protect tourists and foreigners, who are important for the economy. So this complaint was taken seriously. But more serious for the shopkeeper was the threat that volunteers would boycott his shop.

The minibus was just starting off back to camp when the shopkeeper arrived to own up and apologise. He stood on the step, pulling his earlobes as a mark of repentance, and appealed to Vishal in Hindi. But Vishal remained firm and insisted that the volunteers would not use his shop again.

Why did he do it? Did he really expect the girls to be tempted by the promise of a blue movie? There is a perception in India, probably fuelled by films and television as well as by the skimpy clothing worn by some tourists, that Western women have loose morals. Perhaps he thought, *What are these girls doing so far from home without a husband or male relative to chaperone them? Are they on the lookout for sex?*

Many Indian women face harassment, discrimination and worse. I read in the *Times of India* of cases of rape, violence against women and the 'accidental' death of a young wife in a kitchen fire. The domestic incidents were often associated with demands by the woman's in-laws for more dowry, and if she died the man could marry again and receive a large new dowry in addition to retaining the one that his dead wife had provided. But I was never treated with anything but respect and friendliness, nor had the young volunteers complained of unacceptable behaviour on their outings to Jaipur nightclubs.

* * *

The pink paint was peeling on the archway at the school gate, but the long single-storey building, to my left as I entered, was well maintained. A deep pink bougainvillea and a creeper with huge mauve flowers adorned the pink wall of the veranda outside the headmaster's study. Ahead of me, beyond the far wall of the school grounds, stretched fields of lush green crops, and behind them rose low sandy hills. Opposite the main building a grove of trees shaded a garden, where the teachers grew fresh vegetables for the children's lunch. Immediately to the right of the entrance gate was another pink building with a veranda, where I taught seven- and eight-year-olds.

This school was such a contrast to the tiny school where I had taught in the desert. It catered for over two hundred children ranging in age from five to fourteen, who came from several neighbouring villages.

"Our school has won first prize for the best educational standards in the region," one of the teachers told me proudly.

But there were only six teachers for the eight classes, and the headmaster had asked for volunteers to help teach English to the younger children.

The headmaster spoke little English and so one of the other teachers, whose English was reasonably good, liaised with us. One morning he came into my class and congratulated me heartily.

"What for?" I asked.

"The Irish team beat the English in the cricket World Cup, and they broke two world records."

Another day he quizzed me about why I was teaching here.

"Are you a professional?"

"I'm not a professional schoolteacher. I used to lecture in a university," I told him.

However, he persisted in his queries, and I finally realised he wanted to know if I was being paid for what I was doing. I assured him that it was on a purely voluntary basis.

"Is it for personal satisfaction?" he asked, and seemed satisfied when I said it was.

Many people in India find it difficult to understand that anyone would work without being paid, and before coming I had been told to apply for a visitor's visa, because a visa for voluntary work would have been delayed for months. 'Volunteer' is often understood to mean the paid employee of a charitable organisation.

Every morning Máire, Jacqi and I, accompanied by Manoj, would leave our shoes outside under the climber with mauve flowers and sit in the headmaster's study until prayers were over in the big classroom next door, which doubled as a school hall. Manoj told us that, after the prayers to Saraswati, the headmaster said a prayer to the gods of all other religions, including Islam and Christianity. The walls of his study were painted with a variety of pictures. Gandhi and the prime ministers of India rubbed shoulders with Ganesh, Saraswati and other gods and heroes, and amongst them all was a picture of a Swiss chalet in European mountain scenery. Framed certificates and an array of cups attested to the school's high standards. High on one wall was an inscription in Hindi which read, in translation, 'Do today's work today'.

As we walked across to our classroom when prayers were over, one of the boys would offer to carry my bag, and several of the girls would hang on to my hands and arms. One of them tested me every morning:

"What is my name?"

"Shanta," I would reply, and she would beam with satisfaction.

Máire, Jacqi and I were assigned a classroom in which to teach class III. It was a big room, with windows looking out towards the village. There were shelves in alcoves, a blackboard at either end, and maps and a lot of lists in Hindi painted on the walls. The room belonged to a senior class, which was displaced, with their teacher, to the veranda outside. When there were no volunteers, third class shared one of the bigger classrooms with first and second classes.

We divided the thirty or so children between us, and each group was arranged in a row in front of a blackboard. Máire and Jacqi had the blackboards mounted on the walls at either end, and I had one propped up against the wall opposite the windows. The children sat on mats on the floor, but in this school they had little low desks in front of them, which made it much easier for them to write.

Shanta was an enthusiastic member of my group, but her powers of concentration were limited. It was a great achievement when she finally managed to write her own name in Roman letters without help. Shanta sat next to Kiran and was inclined to distract her. Kiran was a head taller than any of the others and must have been a couple of years older, but she did not know how old she was, and the teacher was not sure of her age either. She was keen to learn, though she did not find it easy. Sushila and Asha were two of the younger ones, only just seven years old. But they were both very bright little girls, and indeed Asha was much the cleverest child in the whole class. Rakesh was a small, tough, but very engaging little boy, who was inclined to get into fights with some of the others. He would often arrive in class and show me a bandaged knee or hand.

My group were very good at arithmetic.

"Do addition and subtraction with them but not multiplication and division – they are on next year's syllabus," I was told by the teacher.

So, to make arithmetic more interesting I gave them shopping problems. One day I told them that they each had twenty rupees and I was selling bananas for five rupees each – rather expensive, as

I realised afterwards when I bought a whole bunch for that price. I wanted them to tell me what change they would get if they bought one banana, but my Hindi and their English were not quite up to this. The teacher arrived just as they put their hands up to answer my question, and he said:

"They are all saying they can buy four bananas."

He and I were both very impressed that they had, in effect, done a division sum, even though they had never been taught division or multiplication.

Discipline was strict there, though I never saw a teacher hit a child. But one day I made Asha stand outside the door for a short while because she was being disruptive, and she disappeared. One of the teachers had seen her standing there and sent her to the headmaster. She returned to class in tears, though not, as far as I could tell, physically punished. But I did not make any child stand outside again.

Perhaps it was the large size of this school that led to fights among the children and punishments from those in charge. It was certainly harder to keep control than in the small desert school. Having three groups in one room, all learning essentially the same material, meant that some children would wander away from their own group if they thought that something more interesting was happening at another side of the room. Asha was particularly bad in this regard, as she always finished her worksheet before everyone else and went off to see what the other groups were doing.

But these children could be very kind. One morning Rakesh brought in a much bigger, older boy with a withered arm, and they sat down together. When I handed out worksheets Rakesh indicated that I should give one to the other boy too. The child sat quietly and covered his paper with rows of tiny circles. Whenever he appeared in my class the other children were very gentle with him. He was unable to speak, but if I handed him a worksheet or a piece of paper to write on he rewarded me with a beautiful smile.

He was not, officially, a pupil at the school, but followed the other children in and liked to sit in class with them. The only time he was a nuisance was one day when I was writing on the board, and he stood so close beside me, watching, that I kept tripping over him. The teacher from the class outside on the veranda noticed and came in and gently ushered him out.

The children had no break before lunchtime, but one of the senior boys would come round at mid morning with little china cups of *chai* for the volunteers. Half an hour before the end of morning school we would clear the centre of the room, so that the whole class could join in singing and playing games. Rakesh was always ready to suggest a song and start it off. His favourite was 'The Wheels on the Bus go round and round', and we improvised lots of new verses for it.

When the minibus appeared the children would run to the window crying "Yellow bus, yellow bus", before forming a circle to sing the 'Goodbye Song'. As we left, some of the senior girls walked to the gate with us, wanting to practise their English.

The first question was always, "What is your name?", and then it would be, "What is your father's name?", "What is your brother's name?"

A person's name identifies their status in the caste system. It was never the names of female relatives which they asked for. Sometimes they progressed to, "What is your date of birth?"

(They never asked my age directly.) I would not answer that but told them that I was a grandmother.

* * *

English conversation classes in the afternoons, at a school in another small farming village, were chaotic. I would sit on the floor with half a dozen children crouched around me, while four other volunteers took similar groups in other spots around the dark and dusty classroom. The children ranged from ten to twelve years old, and the noise level made conversation difficult. Manoj had little success in quietening them. Children often moved from one group to another – sometimes several times in an afternoon – but two girls, Angeli and Lali, always stayed with me. Discipline seemed lax in this school, and the staff had little interest in what we did.

"How many brothers do you have and how many sisters?" I asked the children in my group.

"Three sisters, one younger, one older," came the reply from one of the girls.

"Then you have two sisters."

"No, three sisters," she insisted, counting. "Older – one, younger – two, and me – three," pointing at herself.

They always gave the total number of girls, or boys, in the family. I could never persuade them to see the number in relation to themselves instead of to the family as a whole.

I brought along books to read with them, and Dinesh, in my group, had good enough English to read a first Ladybird reader. One book I showed them caused consternation and embarrassment among the girls. It taught the English words for things European children would meet at home and in school. One page showed items of clothing, all individually labelled – trousers, T-shirts, dresses, and so on. But in the middle of the page were two children, a boy and a girl, in their underclothes. Angeli and Lali gazed in horror, and Lali hurriedly turned over to the next page.

A tale of Indian gods and flying elephants was much more successful. After we had read through it a couple of times I decided it was time for drawing, so handed out paper and crayons. But several of the children spent the rest of the afternoon writing out the story word for word and copying the colourful illustrations.

An attractive and happy three year-old-girl lived in a house opposite the school, and she liked to join the class. So we picked her up as we arrived and carried her into the schoolyard, where green parakeets perched and squabbled in a rather sad-looking tree with lopped branches and few leaves. She would point to the sky, the tree and the birds and tell us their names in her own language. Inside she sat on a volunteer's lap and listened quietly to what was going on. She might change laps occasionally, but she was always quiet and never interrupted the lesson. She loved it when we all sat round in a big circle to play a game. Occasionally she would fall asleep during the afternoon, and then Manoj would carry her home, still fast asleep, when the class ended.

On the afternoon before Saraswati's feast day we arrived to find our class cancelled and the whole school assembled outside. We were invited to join the celebration in preparation for the next day's festival, and sat with the teachers on plastic chairs along one side of a raised platform in the open air. One of the older girls came to place a dab of red powder on each of our foreheads.

The older boys were playing cricket, but one of them was persuaded to come and play a drum to accompany the singing. A group of five senior girls, about fourteen years old, led the performance of traditional songs – probably hymns to Saraswati, though nobody explained them to us. Then two of the girls danced very elegantly, in their uniforms of sky blue tunic over white trousers, with a long white scarf draped across the shoulders. They danced, weaving patterns with their arms and hands, and every so often one or both girls would whirl round so that their scarves flew out on either side. But they seemed to have no problem in controlling and retaining them.

The boy on the drum managed to escape to the cricket, and one of the masters took over. He tried to get some of the boys to dance, but the only one who would do so was one of my class who had great self-confidence, though he was rather small for his age. He danced with bent knees and great stamping of feet and wriggling of hips, to much applause. At the end one of the senior girls came round with a bag of small white sweets which she distributed to everyone.

The families of the children I taught were farmers, owning animals and growing crops on a much larger scale than the subsistence farming around Shiv. But they were still very poor, and there were no cars and no television aerials to be seen in the village.

I enjoyed walking the two kilometres back to camp, and the other volunteers usually preferred to walk rather than wait for the minibus. Manoj did not like walking but felt it his duty to stay with us, and he trailed along in the rear.

The village houses were single-storeyed, some whitewashed and others painted blue or pink. The front door opened onto a courtyard, and usually there were no windows. Some had cow pats drying on the roof for use as fuel, and cows and water buffalo were tethered outside. Goats, chickens and hairy pigs roamed the street. One family was prosperous enough to have six young cows beside their house, and a small plot behind, where wheat was growing.

There were no shops apart from a small *chai* stall. At the village pump several of the girls who had led the singing for Saraswati's feast day were fetching water as we walked home, and they called to us and posed for photographs. The pump was always a centre of activity in any village. Women and girls chatted as they filled their pots. On one occasion a man taking a shower, dressed only in shorts, waved to me cheerfully and posed to be photographed, while three women carrying water pots looked on, one with her face veiled with her diaphanous red scarf.

On the edge of the village were two small muddy ponds. Waterfowl hid beneath the bushes at the water's edge, red-legged stilts paddled, and little brown herons fished, flying up with a flash of white wings as we approached. When we had passed the last houses the road ran between fields of mustard. Then we reached the main road, with the Snake Charmers' settlement and our camp on the far side.

As we walked through the village the families of some of the children we taught invited us in. They would pull down a *palang* for us to sit on and, while the woman of the house prepared *chai* for us, friends and neighbours would crowd into the courtyard. Once again I noticed that a woman veiled her face in the presence of her father-in-law and uncovered it again when he left. When we said goodbye, the woman of the house would often bring out a plate with red powder and rice grains on it. She would place a red mark on each of our foreheads and press a few rice grains onto it.

One of my pupils, whose house we were visiting, pointed to some of the other children and explained:

"He is my brother, and that one is my real brother."

'Brother' can mean a cousin as well as a sibling. One of the boys asked my age, so as usual I said I was a *dadi*. He reported this to his father, who clearly did not believe it. When I explained (in my best Hindi) that I had two sons, two daughters-in-law and a *poti* (granddaughter) he said, according to Manoj:

"Perhaps she might be as much as fifty years old."

The Indians always underestimated my age, which was flattering and made me feel re-tyred rather than retired.

I was amused to see rather macho young boys from my class carrying their baby brothers around and taking good care of them. The babies always had their eyes rimmed with black kohl. The boys seemed to be just as good with younger children as the girls were. Their politeness and friendliness impressed me too, and the easy way they could chat to me even though I was of their grandparents' generation. On one occasion a group of teenage boys walked with me, and talked to me, practising their English. I was touched when, on parting, they thanked me very politely for talking to them.

We were invited into one courtyard where an old man dressed all in white sat on a *palang*. His grandson, one of our pupils, was there with some of his friends. The old man and his wife talked to Manoj but did not offer us *chai*, and Manoj explained afterwards that they were extremely poor, even poorer than the other villagers. They had five sons, who had all gone away to find work in the city, so the old couple had no men to help with the farm work. Although some men do well enough in the city to send money home to relatives left behind, many can only just manage to scrape a living.

An elderly lady standing outside her house hailed us as we walked by one day. She had no relations attending the school, but she wanted to entertain us. She was very proud of her house as it was new, only completed a few weeks before. It had two front doors and over each was a decorative panel showing Ganesh. She brought out a *palang* for us to sit on in the courtyard and offered us *chai*. We accepted, but then were dismayed to see her give a pot and some money to a girl and tell her to fetch *chai* from the *chai* stall. Manoj offered to pay, but she refused. She said it was an honour to have us there to visit her.

Dinesh often accompanied us as far as his home, which was at the very end of the village. He always wanted us to come and take *chai* with his family. Usually Manoj said no, we must get back to camp. However, one day we arrived to find that the children had been given a half day's holiday – apparently because it was the end of the month, though it was not clear whether this happened every month. Dinesh saw the minibus arriving and ran up to say:

"Today you must come to my house."

His family was taken by surprise, but they were very hospitable. Two young women were busy outside as we approached, but they dropped what they were doing and brought us through to a courtyard at the back. All the family gathered round, including Dinesh's older brother, younger sister, parents and grandfather. One of the young women was an unmarried aunt. They gave us *chai* and talked to Manoj for a long time. The father was very interested in his children's education, but I could not take part in the conversation and had to rely on Manoj to translate.

On these house visits I longed to be able to speak Hindi. Although I could exchange information about children and grandchildren with the woman of the house, I always had to rely on Manoj as interpreter for any other topic. This was very restricting, as Manoj could not often interrupt the conversation to explain it to me. It made me determined to learn the language.

* * *

The state of the road between Dausa and Lalsot was appalling. It was full of pot holes, the margins were perilously soft, and in some places the surface had vanished altogether.

"It's like that because of the corruption of local politicians," I was told. "They offer to repair small stretches in exchange for votes, and it is not in their interests to maintain the whole road properly."

My first experience of this road was on my arrival from Jaipur, after the inaugural week at the volunteer headquarters. The camp minibus bounced and bumped along, and I began to feel very travel sick. Kirti had come to collect me at Dausa, to greet me and bring me to Lalsot camp.

"Welcome!" she shouted, and she began to tell me about the camp. But I could hear little of what she said above the rattling and banging of the minibus.

The fifty-kilometre drive took an hour and a half, provided there were no punctures or other emergencies. Later, when I went to Jaipur for the weekend, I would insist that the taxi take the alternative route from Lalsot. Although it was a smaller road, and avoided the long stretch of excellent tolled highway from Dausa to Jaipur, it was a more comfortable drive. But on weekend excursions further afield it was impossible to avoid the drive between Lalsot and Dausa.

The road was very busy as well as uncomfortable, and accidents and punctures were inevitable. On one occasion a bus in front of us sank a rear wheel into the soft ground at the edge, as it tried to overtake a lorry on the inside, and was brought to a stop in a precarious position tilting over on the edge of a shallow drop. Another time a lorry, stopped by a puncture, blocked the very middle of the road. On the way home one Sunday evening our car had a puncture. As Thea and I stood beside the road, local children and a woman came to chat to us, while our driver, cheerful as ever, changed the wheel.

Once, when Thea and I were on the way to catch a train at Dausa, our taxi was stopped at a bend in the road as we left Lalsot. One heavy lorry travelling towards Dausa was overtaking another, and several cars, including our taxi, moved out to overtake them and found there was no way through. As the road was only three lanes wide this blocked it completely to any traffic coming in the opposite direction. But none of the drivers appeared upset or impatient. They turned off their engines, got out to survey the situation ahead, and stood and chatted to one another.

"Is there an accident?" I asked our driver.

"No, just a traffic jam."

The road beyond the bend was also blocked, by vehicles three abreast coming towards us, so there was no way through in either direction. Eventually somebody worked out a plan, and our taxi and the other cars in the same lane backed onto the right-hand verge so that traffic coming into Lalsot could get through slowly in single file. Finally the traffic leaving Lalsot could move, though as our taxi was on the wrong side of the road it took some time before we got going again. In spite of the long delay we caught our train – it was late too.

"I saved a life yesterday," our taxi driver told us as we returned after a weekend break. "I drove from Lalsot to Dausa in thirty-five minutes."

"What happened? An accident?"

"No," he replied. "It was a pregnant woman who was bleeding heavily. She needed to get to the hospital in Dausa quickly."

That drive always took us at least three times as long, so the poor woman must have had a dreadful journey. Not surprisingly the car had suffered too, and we had to stop at a pump while the driver topped up the cooling system.

There was one final adventure on this road, on the night that I left Lalsot to return home. The moon was full and bright when we left camp in the minibus at three o'clock in the morning of the day when Holi was to be celebrated. We had not even reached Lalsot when we were stopped by a group of young men wielding big sticks, who had placed rocks across the road. They wanted money, but cleared the way for us after Ravi handed over a couple of notes. Then, on the potholed road beyond Lalsot, we came across two more roadblocks. Our driver cleverly evaded the first by taking to the verge on the inside of a big lorry that the men were holding up. But we could not avoid the second. A minibus full of Europeans might have seemed a tempting target for thieves, but once again the men merely argued briefly with Ravi before taking away the rocks so that we could move on. These young men were probably local lads, trying to raise enough money to celebrate Holi with colours – and alcohol – later in the morning.

* * *

I had kept in touch with Hitesh by phone and email. He had resigned from the volunteer organisation soon after I left Shiv.

"I need a better paid job," he explained.

But it was not easy to get work as a guide, and his employment with the volunteer organisation was not recognised as appropriate experience. He decided that he would have a better chance if he learnt another language and had already started teaching himself German. By the time I arrived in Lalsot he was taking a German course at a college in Pune.

Camel carts and a moped on the road in Rajasthan.

Cranes beside a pool provided for them by local villagers.

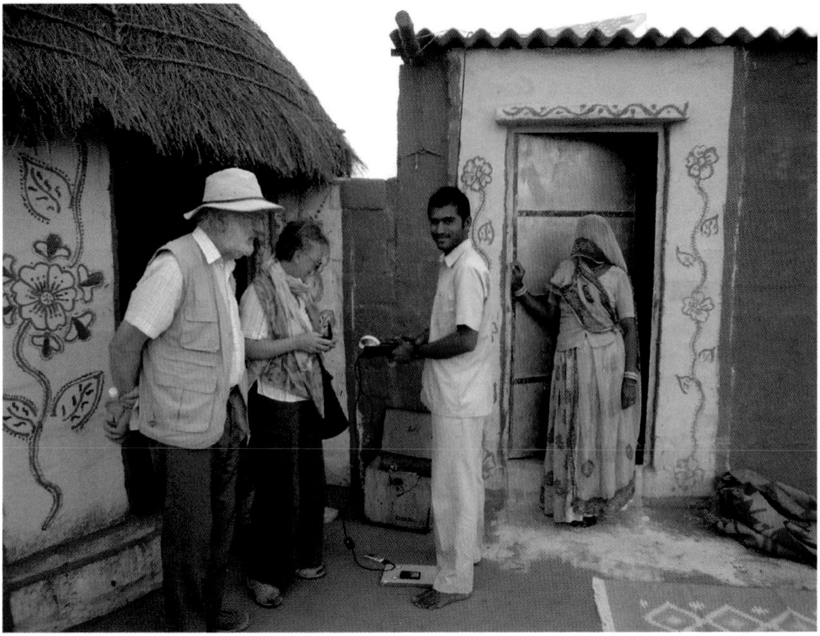

Paying for a duri with a credit card using a car battery and a mobile phone.

The Thar desert with Jaisalmer Fort on its rocky outcrop.

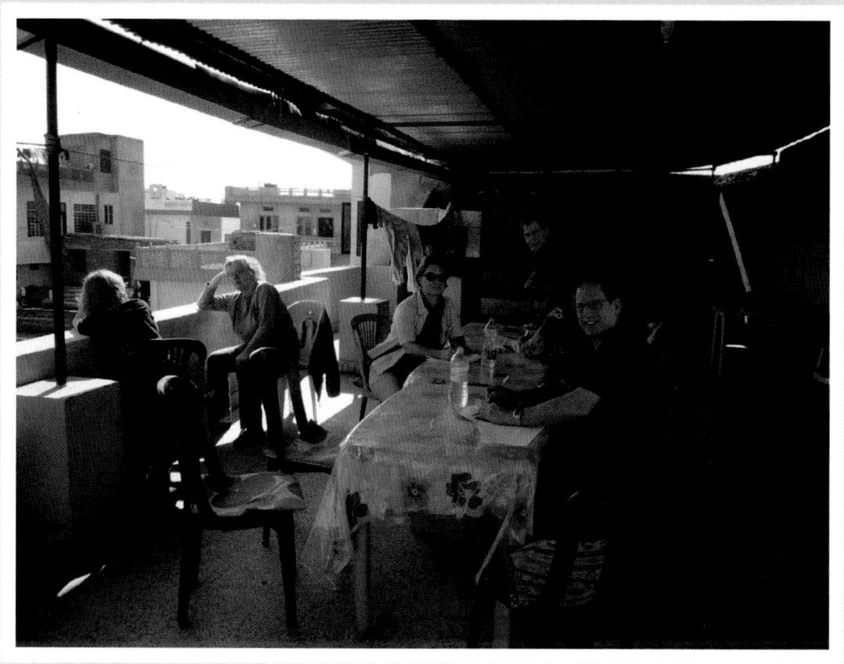

Lunch on the roof at the volunteer headquarters in Jaipur.

Shiv camp.

Shiv camp: washing up behind the dining hall.

Shiv camp: preparing lessons in the recreation hall.

The village buildings in the distance as we drive to the school across the desert.

Break time.

Stalls beside the main road through Shiv.

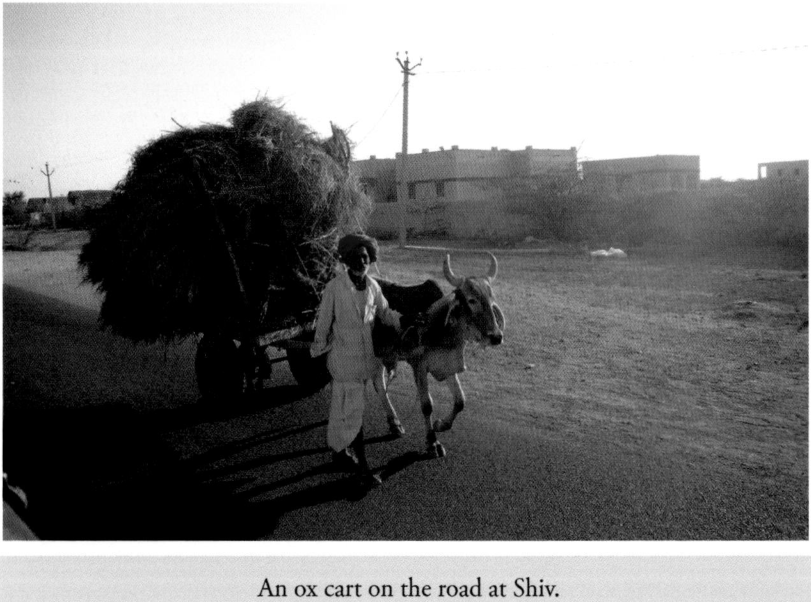

An ox cart on the road at Shiv.

A temple at Khajuraho, with four spires like a mountain range, representing four stages of life.

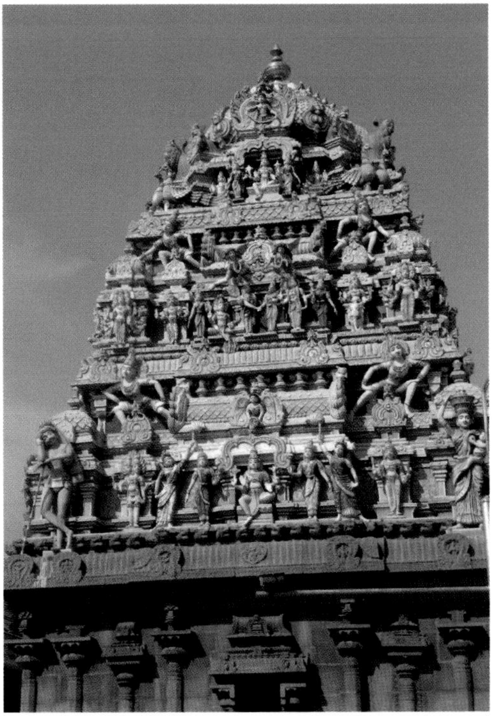

The single spire of a southern Indian temple.

A country road near Lalsot.

Entering the school near Lalsot where I taught in the mornings.

A village house with cow pats drying on the roof.

A village pump.

Water buffalo in the village near Lalsot where I taught in the afternoons.

A visit to the home of one of my pupils.

View from the volunteer house near Bundla village.

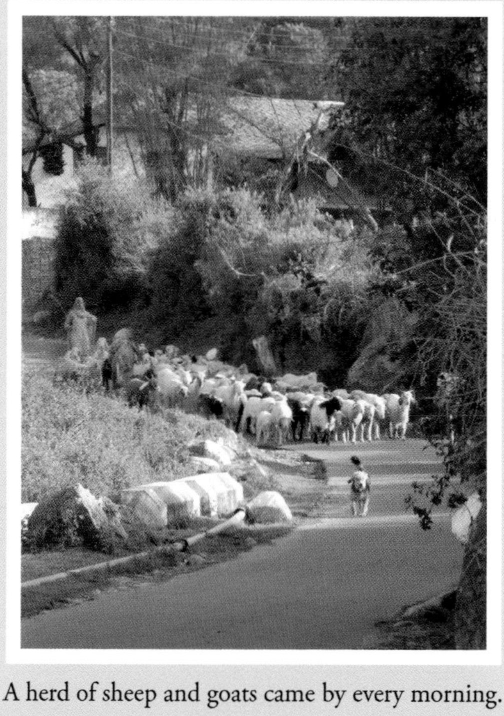

A herd of sheep and goats came by every morning.

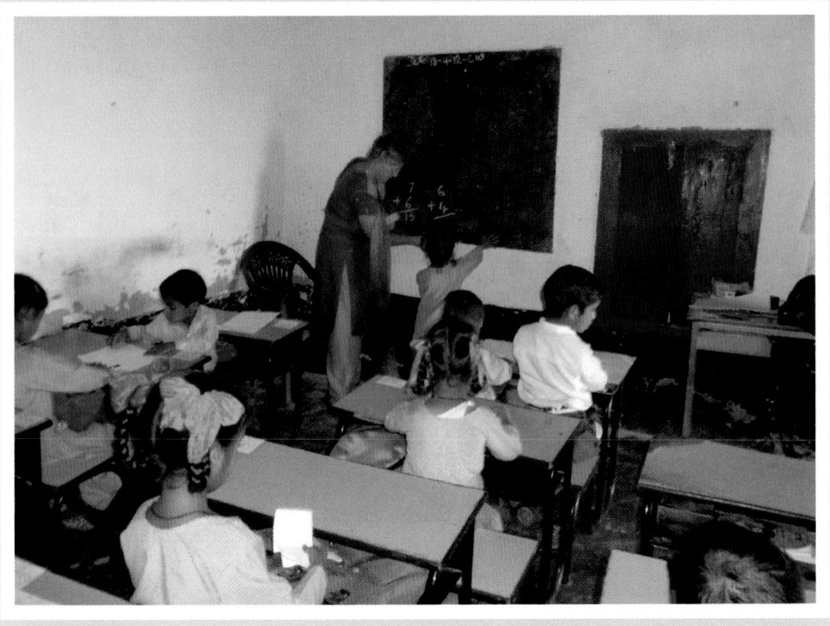

Teaching maths in the Bundla village school.

A school outing.

Waiting for a taxi at the fork in Bundla village.

Women picking tea outside Palampur.

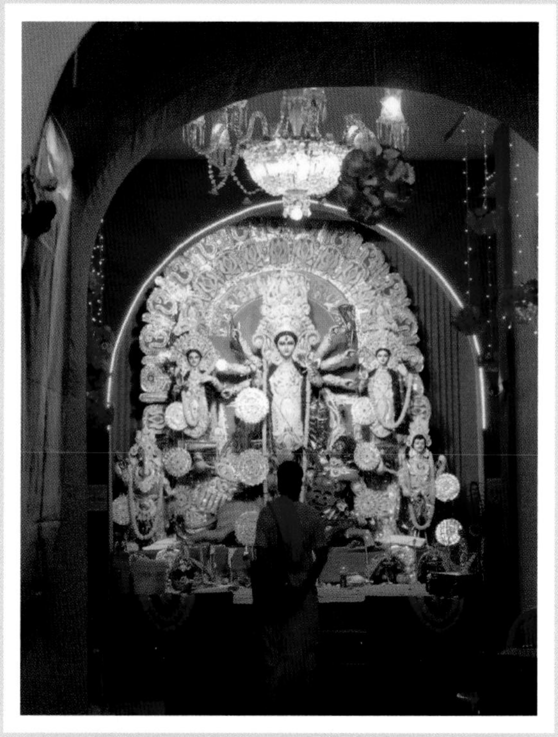

Our local Durga pandal in Kolkata.

The lake where Durga was immersed,
covered with the detritus of other Durgas.

Goats and chickens beside the big main road near my apartment in Kolkata.

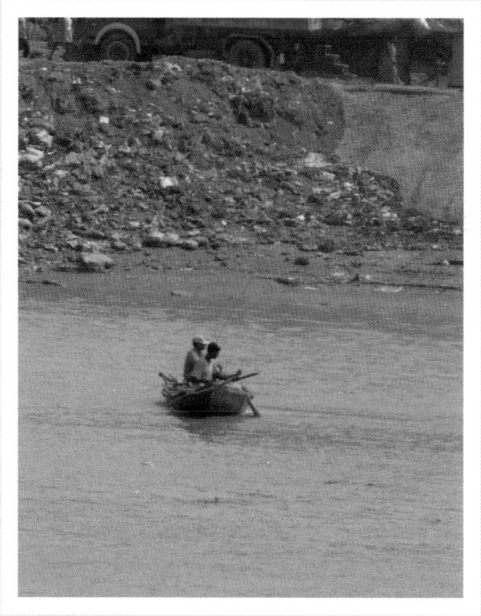

Men fishing on the Hooghly, in front of a rubbish tip.

Weighing petals in the wholesale flower market.

Street fireworks at Divali.

His parents had found out about his girlfriend. He had confided in his sister-in-law, and she eventually explained to them why he would not let them find him a wife. The family all felt he should give her up, and repeated stories of local boys who had been driven to suicide when their Western girlfriends went home and failed to keep in contact. His father was very upset and said:

"The worst mistake I ever made was to give you a higher education."

It was extremely upsetting for Hitesh, as he is very close to his family and very fond of them. But his dreams still centred on being able, one day, to marry his girlfriend. She was no less serious about him, and they communicated every day, he in India and she in Europe, through the internet.

* * *

Breakfasting on the rooftop of our hotel in Udaipur, Thea and I gazed in awe at the massive palace complex, with its ornate turrets, descending in layers of ochre stone to the lake's edge. The water glittered in the early morning light. In the opposite direction rose the white tower of a temple, covered with intricate carvings. Between this temple and the palace a crowd of monkeys basked in the morning sunshine on the ochre tower of another temple.

Now that I was back in India, Hitesh had invited me to visit his family in Udaipur and to bring a friend with me. So Thea and I had braved the drive from Lalsot to Dausa and an overnight train journey, to arrive at six o'clock in the morning at Udaipur station, where Hitesh greeted me with a big hug.

After settling into a hotel (Hitesh had to thunder on the door and phone them up to get us let in at that early hour) Thea and I breakfasted and then wandered round the narrow streets. We gazed out from a lakeside *ghat*, in the company of several cows and a woman washing clothes. I peered through the ornate gates to the hotel buildings where I had stayed in luxury two years before, but with no desire to return to the pampered life of a tourist. Then we met Hitesh near the foot of the marble steps up to the white temple, where two women sat with baskets of bright pink and white flowers at their feet, making garlands for worshippers to buy.

Hitesh led us uphill and down, through narrow streets and lanes, to his home. As we approached, a large white cow that had been sitting outside got up and moved away. He said:

"My mother feeds it a chapati every morning and evening."

On either side of the smart wooden front door the wall was decorated with the traditional swastika sign for good luck, with below it a painting of a woman carrying a pot with coconut leaves sprouting from the top.

The house was tall and narrow. We were greeted on the first floor by Hitesh's mother, a small homely woman, and his elder sister-in-law.

"My younger sister lives here too," Hitesh said, "and my younger sister-in-law. She has just had her first baby."

They were not introduced to us, and the menfolk were out at work. Hitesh explained that, as the family increased, they had built extra floors, and he took us up more stairs until we emerged on the roof. From here we looked over a jumble of houses, each with its flat roof, some with brightly coloured washing left out to dry, and Hitesh pointed out the house where his uncle, aunt and cousins lived, just a stone's throw away.

In Hitesh's own room we were seated on chairs in front of a coffee table, while Hitesh sat on the end of his bed. It was a big room, with a cheerful scarlet cover on the bed and a TV set in front of a curtained area.

"I keep all my books behind the curtain," Hitesh told us.

A small boy peered round the door and, encouraged by Hitesh, came in to the room and was introduced:

"This is my three year-old-nephew."

He was very shy, but clearly delighted to have his uncle home, and he had a great time throwing himself onto the bed from a shelf along the wall behind it. He was already at school. Hitesh had persuaded his brother and sister-in-law that the child should be sent to a good private school which taught through English, to give him the best education and chance in life.

Hitesh's mother and elder sister-in-law cooked us an appetising lunch, consisting of several different little dishes of dal and vegetables on a tray, with very good chapatis and spicy papadums made with gram flour. They did not eat with us, but his mother stayed while we ate, and once again I wished I knew enough Hindi to be able to talk to her.

After our lunch a woman looked in and greeted us as she left the house.

"She comes in every day to massage my sister-in-law and provide her with special strengthening food, because it's only a few weeks since she had her baby," Hitesh said.

His mother brought her latest grandson in to show us, and asked me to wash my hands at the sink in the hall so that I could hold him. The little thing gazed at me with big wide-open eyes, and the new mother smiled at us from outside the room.

From the house we had heard the hammering from the workshop just down the street, where Hitesh's father beat sheets of brass into water pots. As we left we stopped to say "*Namaste*" at the open door of the workshop. Hitesh's father, a handsome man with a shock of black hair, worked a twelve-hour day. He arrived home that evening, just as Thea and I were leaving after another tasty meal prepared for us by Hitesh's mother and sister-in-law.

* * *

Hitesh wanted us to see the sights of Udaipur, and we climbed a small hill beside Lake Pichola to watch the sun set. There was a cable car to the top, and Hitesh asked solicitously whether I would like to go up that way. But I preferred to walk, and watch the tiny purple sunbirds fluttering from blossom to blossom and the macaque monkeys peering at us from the trees. There was a small temple at the top, to a local goddess, where we removed our shoes, and Hitesh said a private prayer. Thea and I watched a little squirrel trying to join in the feast of grain that the priest had laid out for the temple's white mice.

We sat on the terrace near the top of the cable car as the sun sank behind the Aravalli hills, making a golden path across the waters of the lake and leaving streamers of pink cloud in the sky. The lights began to come on in the city below, and all was quiet and peaceful.

The next day Hitesh took us through the old market, where spices and grains were displayed in open sacks. The green powder in one sack was henna, which, when mixed with water, makes the dark brown paste used to pattern the hands and arms of women – a kind of temporary tattoo. A man was selling brown lumps of something from a barrow.

"It is jaggery – it comes from sugar cane," Hitesh explained.

Women sat on the ground selling leafy green stalks with little round seed pods on the end.

"That's fresh gram. The mature pods become chick peas, and they can be ground up to make gram flour."

He took us to one of his family's three shops, where they sold the water pots his father made as well as other metal kitchen and table ware. We were introduced to an older brother who was looking after the shop. In the interval between leaving Shiv and enrolling at Pune, Hitesh had worked there. His father would have liked him to have joined the family business, but Hitesh was determined to find a job where he could use his college training and his ability with languages. However, whenever he was at home for any length of time he felt it his duty to help (without pay) in the family shops.

The big concrete building to which Hitesh took us for lunch looked rather unprepossessing but was a popular eating place for Udaipurans. It was far from any tourist areas, and Thea and I were the only white people in the *thali* restaurant on the first floor. (*Thali* literally means a plate.) We followed other diners in washing our hands in the basin at one side of the room before sitting down to eat. Although the restaurant was very busy Hitesh had managed to get us a table to ourselves. Other diners sat wherever there was space, at long communal tables.

This meal was a completely new eating experience. A big stainless steel plate with six or seven little bowls on it was placed in front of each of us. There was no menu – *thali* was a fixed meal. One waiter came round carrying a set of four serving pots containing different vegetable curries, and placed a ladleful of each into four of our bowls. Then other waiters placed a curd with some little seeds in it in one bowl, a dal in another, and a big spoonful of basmati rice, a spicy papadum, two little round puffed *puris* and a light chapati directly onto the tray. Finally we were each given a stainless steel mug of buttermilk. Each dish was differently spiced, providing a variety of flavours. The buttermilk was a cooling contrast to the spices, though none of the food was too hot for my taste. As we ate, the waiters came round to top up any of our bowls that looked empty and to offer us more rice or chapati. In the last bowl we were given a sweet coconut concoction to finish the meal.

Before catching the overnight train that evening we had time to walk beside Fatehsagar Lake just outside the city.

"This is a favourite place for Udaipurans to come and stroll in the evenings," Hitesh said.

Wooded slopes descended to the lake on all sides, and there were few buildings. Like Lake Pichola, Fatehsagar is an artificial lake, created over three hundred years ago. An elegant promenade lies along the top of the dam which controls the flow of water down to Lake Pichola.

"If you had been here at this time last year," Hitesh told us, "you would not have seen any water. The monsoon was poor the summer before, and Lake Pichola turned into a green meadow, where flocks of goats and sheep could graze."

* * *

"You should go and visit the Maharaja's palace while you're there," said Amitabh, who had arranged a weekend trip for me. "I have told them you are coming."

And so, after several weeks spent teaching the children of small-scale farmers and visiting their homes, I went to visit a maharaja, at the opposite end of the social scale.

I had wandered around the museums and public rooms in maharajas' palaces in Jaipur and Udaipur, and even stayed in hotels which were part of a palace, but I had never actually met a maharaja before.

In the days of the princely states the maharajas were absolute rulers of their regions and fabulously wealthy. Their palaces were extravagantly decorated and furnished; they wore gorgeous robes and magnificent jewels. One collected Rolls Royces, another was a fan of the railways. He had the tracks extended so that he and his guests could alight at the main doorway of his palace, and he served drinks from a miniature train which ran around his enormous dining table, stopping long enough for a guest to help himself from one of the decanters in its trucks.

What did Indian independence mean to the maharajas? Many people feared that, when the British left, India would fragment – the maharajas would refuse to join the new state and would set themselves up as independent rulers. In his book on the history of modern India[6], Ramachandra Guha relates how Vallabhbhai Patel was appointed to persuade them that their future must be as part of the new India.

6 *India after Gandhi* by Ramachandra Guha, Macmillan 2007.

Helped by Lord Mountbatten, the last viceroy, who warned that Britain would not recognise or support independent princedoms, he convinced nearly all of them. But the Maharaja of Kashmir held out until after Independence. Straddling the new Pakistan-India border, Kashmir had a large population of Muslims, but the Maharaja was Hindu. The Punjab had been split in two at partition, the northern part going to Pakistan and the southern to India. But the Maharaja's stance prevented this solution for Kashmir. It was only after an armed force of tribesmen from the neighbouring area of Pakistan invaded Kashmir in the autumn of 1947, several months after Independence, that he called for the help of the Indian army and fled to the Hindu area of Jammu. Kashmir became part of India, but the Maharaja's intransigence left a lasting legacy of unrest and violence in the region.

I was driven along streets lined by respectable but unexceptional houses, and then suddenly on the right was a great gateway and beyond it the sparklingly white turrets and domes of the palace. We approached along a driveway paved in pink stone, with a row of small fountains down the centre and smooth green lawns bordered by flowering shrubs on either side. Brilliant pink bougainvillea cascaded over an elegant white archway, beneath which a very small girl was playing with a very large drum, almost as big as herself, watched over by a smartly dressed young man.

Like many others when their annual stipend from the government was cancelled by Indira Gandhi, the Maharaja had opened part of his palace as a luxury hotel. The manager met me and called for coffee to be served. We sat in comfortable wicker chairs at a table in an open courtyard, surrounded on three sides by wings of the palace. Above each door and window were panels elaborately painted with twining green foliage and orange flowers, and orange chrysanthemums in pots surrounded a small fountain in the centre of the courtyard.

"That was the Maharaja's granddaughter you saw as you came in," the manager told me. "She is two years old."

"Can she inherit the title, or is it only for sons?"

"Not even the Maharaja's son can inherit the title now," he replied. "The titles have been abolished. But of course everyone round here knows the family and will respect them even without the title."

He showed me round some of the beautifully furnished hotel rooms, and a great dining hall in a new building on the far side of an open-air swimming pool. It had been erected to cater for increased numbers of hotel guests, in exactly the same style as the old palace, with huge glass chandeliers hanging from the high ceiling and pictures of past maharajas on the walls.

As we walked back through the grounds he stopped near a gap in a well-trimmed hedge.

"Wait a moment," he said, as he disappeared through the gap.

A minute later he reappeared and beckoned me through to meet a tall, distinguished-looking man in Western-style shirt and trousers.

"Do join us," said the Maharaja.

He and his wife were relaxing in their private garden, separated from the public path by the hedge. Decorative trees showed fresh green foliage, and roses were in full bloom in the flower beds. The manager withdrew, and I was offered a chair. The Maharaja's wife, in a lovely sari patterned all over in a pink floral design, said little as the Maharaja engaged me in conversation.

I admired the garden.

"Last winter was the coldest we've ever had," he replied. "It got down to two degrees below freezing, and my mango tree died. The roses were damaged too, but I've managed to save them."

He asked me about my volunteering work and about Ireland.

"I have never been there, but I have visited England many times."

It amused him when I explained that the island had been partitioned on independence, like India.

He told me a little about the governance of his state.

"We elect seven members to the Rajasthan state government. That government then sends representatives to the Indian federal parliament."

The maharajas lost their political power at Independence, though one might be democratically elected if he stood for a seat in government. Now tourism is one way of providing an income to help keep them in the style to which they are accustomed.

"We always go to Europe in the autumn," the Maharaja said, "to attend a big annual tourism conference."

After half an hour of pleasant conversation I said goodbye to the Maharaja and his wife and went to find my driver. He had remained in the car park all that time and was asleep in his car.

* * *

The weather was very hot during my last week at Lalsot. Although it did not reach forty degrees I felt hotter than I ever had at Shiv, because this area is more humid. We even had a thunderstorm one morning, when it rained heavily for an hour, leaving great puddles across the camp. At school the summer schedule began, with classes starting and finishing an hour earlier. The number of children at my afternoon class dropped, as the school was closed for the day, and classrooms locked, by the time we got there. But many of the class came, and we played games with them in the shade of the veranda.

The last afternoon class was on Thursday. Several of my group said to me:

"You go aeroplane – no!"

Angeli was really sad, and she and her friend offered to go in the aeroplane with me.

It is traditional for volunteers to give the children chocolate when they leave, and word had got round the village. So we were besieged by crowds of children, including teenagers, who had nothing to do with our class. We tried to hand out chocolates to our own pupils, but there was such a stampede that we had to give up, and some of them did not get any, or had theirs taken away by bigger children. The three-year-old who liked coming to our class had to be picked up and carried, as she was in danger of being squashed in the crowd. We were rescued from the mob by the Indian woman who ran the local daycare centre, whose youngest daughter was in our class. She took us to her house, where, unusually, her front courtyard had a high gate. She shut the gate and we sat in the courtyard drinking *chai* until our minibus arrived, while a crowd of children outside peered in at us through the railings of the gate.

The next morning at school was a more organised affair. The children were much too excited for lessons, but we had arranged a drawing and colouring competition, and then a game of ten-pin bowling. The skittles were made from empty plastic water bottles, with sand in the base to stabilise them. The older children and their teacher from the class on the veranda stood at the door to watch, and one of the girls came in to sit by the bottles and set them up again when they were knocked down. We made it a competition between the girls and the boys. (There was only one more boy than girls in our class.) The boys won at skittles. Then we had a hopping relay race up and down the classroom. Luckily the girls won this time, and so each child in the class received one of the little medals that Máire had brought from Ireland. They were medals Irish primary school children are given for competing in team games, and our children were delighted with them.

At the end of the morning we were asked to sit on the platform in the hall, and the whole school was arrayed in rows on the floor below us. The headmaster spoke in Hindi, and one of the teachers in English. He thanked us for helping in the school and invited us to visit them again next time we were in India. Máire and I each said a few words in reply and told them how much we had enjoyed teaching there. The headmaster presented us each with a statuette of Saraswati and a pen, and one of the senior girls came round to put red marks and grains of rice on our foreheads. Then we gave chocolates to the headmaster to distribute to the children, waved goodbye, and left in the minibus.

* * *

Holi fell on Sunday that year, and we were to leave for Delhi and home that day. Vishal announced that we would celebrate Holi a day early, on Saturday. But we were taken by surprise by the executives on Friday evening. I was typing an email when Giri came into the office and put his hands on my cheeks and said, "Happy Holi", leaving me with bright green powder all over my face. When I went out everyone was throwing red and green powder, and soon all our faces, arms and clothes were coloured. There was time for a shower before dinner, but the colour does not come out of fair hair very easily, so the blond volunteers were left with tasteful green and pink streaks in their hair.

That was just a preview of the real thing, and we were warned to be prepared at ten o'clock the next morning. The traditional way to celebrate is for a couple of friends to visit another friend's house, say 'Happy Holi' and embrace them while putting colour on them. Then that friend joins them and they move on to another friend's house. Gradually a big group builds up, and they start throwing water, and then mud. So on Saturday we all put colour on each other's faces, in a civilised way at first, while Vishal (duly coloured) sat in the shade just inside the recreation room door and played the drum, and the Indians all joined in the singing. Gradually the colour throwing got wilder, and then the executives decided it was water throwing time. The sun had warmed the water from the tank, so it was refreshing to be drenched. The ground became a sandy quagmire, and we all danced in the mud to Indian music from the radio, looking like a lot of savages. But everything came to a stop in time for us to clean ourselves up before lunch.

In the evening after dinner a bonfire was lit and we had a final farewell ceremony. Kirti brought out a dish on which were a little pile of red powder, rice grains, and some pieces of string made of yellow and brown threads twisted together. She performed the *puja* (prayer ceremony) to consecrate these things by walking seven times round the fire, spilling water on the ground from a bottle she carried, and waving the dish in circles in front of the flames. Then she came round to each of us to put a red mark on the forehead, press rice grains onto it and tie one of the strings like a bracelet round one wrist. Finally she handed out the traditional tiny round white sweets.

When I said goodbye to Giri he put his hand to his forehead and then bent down to touch my foot. This is a mark of respect when leaving a parent or senior person. It embarrassed me enormously.

Chapter 6

CASTE AND MARRIAGE

Even on my original visit to India, as a tourist, I had become aware of people who seemed to be excluded from society. It was not so much the hawkers and beggars that drew my attention. They interacted with other people, selling their trinkets or receiving alms. But there were others, low caste workers, who might have been a figment of my imagination for all the notice that was taken of them by the crowds around them.

I visited an elegant Moghul building, crowned by a great dome, with smaller domes and turrets on either side. Delicately inlaid panels, and the white stone outlining its arches, relieved the darkness of its red sandstone. Spread before and around it were beds filled with bright scarlet and white flowers, set between smooth green lawns.

Families out for the day wandered along the paths, the women in beautiful saris chatting to one another, while their children darted here and there in the sunshine. Smartly dressed businessmen hurried by to their appointments, and guides explained the building and its history to groups of tourists. Nobody took any notice of the woman in the faded green and yellow sari. She was bent double, sweeping the path with a broom made from long stems of stiff grass. The crowds passed by, ignoring her as though she did not exist.

In one of the great palaces, along one side of an open courtyard, a row of steps led up to an arched veranda. I gazed out, across a vista of ochre houses and narrow streets below the palace walls, to the desert stretching to the horizon beyond. A woman in a cheap sari squatted on the steps behind me, scrubbing them. She seemed invisible to those admiring the architecture and the view. Like the woman sweeping in the gardens, she was one of the many poor, low caste people, who traditionally perform necessary but menial work all over India.

"Caste does not matter anymore in the cities," said the speaker at one of the inaugural talks for volunteers in the city of Jaipur. "It is only in rural areas that it may still have some importance."

But as we left the lecture room I met a woman coming up the stairs, dressed in a shabby cotton sari and carrying a heavy load of building material. She and her husband were building a new room for the volunteer organisation. They were clearly of low caste, like the women I had seen sweeping the paths and cleaning the steps. Did they feel that caste was of no importance, I wondered. Did they have any option other than to take work that is traditionally allotted to those of low caste? I find it hard to see how caste can cease to be important until jobs such as sweeping the paths, cleaning and heavy labour are divorced from the caste of the worker.

When I mentioned what we had been told in Jaipur to Giri he was dismissive.

"Whatever these city people say, I would be willing to bet anything that they will not marry outside their own caste," he said. "Ninety per cent of marriages are within caste."

He went on to give me a tutorial on the caste system:

"In the Vedas, which are many thousands of years old, people's occupations were classified into four groups. These are classifications, not castes, and each group, or *varna*, contains many castes and subcastes. *Brahmin* is the group of priestly castes which came out of the mouth of Brahma, *Kshatriya* the group of warrior and ruler castes which came from Brahma's shoulders, *Vaisya*, the merchants and businessmen, were born from his stomach, and *Chhudra*, the servants and lower castes, originated in his feet."

But originally a man's family status did not restrict his trade or profession.

"Until about two and a half thousand years ago anyone could choose to become a merchant or a warrior or even a Brahmin," Giri continued. "But the Brahmins did not like this, and restricted entry to the priesthood to those who came from priestly families. From then on the caste into which one was born determined what one's occupation would be. It was at this time, too, that those performing the most menial and dirty jobs were deemed untouchable – lower than the lowest of the *Chhudra*."

"So, how many castes are there?"

"There are as many as fifty different castes, and each of them contains a very large number of subcastes. The status of each family is determined by their name, which indicates their caste and subcaste. The technical skills associated with a person's traditional occupation are passed down through the family. My family were farmers until my father went into business. But he learnt about farming from my grandfather and has passed this knowledge on to my brother and me, even though neither of us intends to become a farmer."

I had already come across families who passed their skills down from father to son: the people in Agra who created beautiful designs in inlaid marble, and the silk weavers in Varanasi.

On a tour in southern India our driver was extremely knowledgeable about local agriculture.

"That field of rice will be ready for harvest in ten days' time," he would tell us, or "These fields will be planted for a third rice crop later this year if the weather is good from now on. But it has been cold, and this first crop is two weeks late."

"How do you know so much about farming?" I asked him.

"My father is a farmer, like my grandfather and his father before him," he explained. "He grows rice and aubergines commercially, and he taught me all about farming."

The book I had been reading on Rajasthani folklore and tradition suggested that the caste system will endure so long as there is no way of acquiring the training for one's trade other than through members of one's own family or caste. Though some castes may train people from outside their group, others restrict training to their own members. If they could obtain training from another caste, those of lower caste might take the opportunity of moving up in the system. It seemed to me that the provision of training in crafts and trades, open to anyone irrespective of their caste, should be as important as giving everyone a basic education.

At home I talked about this to an Irish man who had been a teacher at a good private school in Darjeeling.

"That is not a problem now," he declared. "There are lots of technical colleges in small towns where any young man can be trained in the trade of his choice."

But I thought of the tiny villages I had visited, with no shops, and some with no school. How could a young man from a family living in such a village afford such training? He would have to leave home to go to a town where there was a college, and how would he survive while he was there? His family would lose an important member of their workforce and might not support his desire to learn a different trade from their own. And what about the young women? They are destined to be wives and mothers, and education for them is not a priority in many rural areas. To go away from the village on their own to learn a trade would be unthinkable.

* * *

One of my Irish colleagues returned from a visit to an Indian university and told me that his host there was paying for the education of the son of his servants, who was a very bright boy. A good education can provide opportunities for those from the lower echelons of society. In a city they may, if they are lucky, find employment in offices or businesses and improve their social status. The state offers free education to all children up to the age of fourteen, but the standard of education in government schools is variable, and the village schools where I taught had few resources.

"Caste prejudice remains, in the cities as well as in rural areas," my colleague told me. "My host was able to get a good private school to accept the boy without too much difficulty. But he also insisted that the child's name must be changed. If he used his real family name he would inevitably have been recognised as low caste and discriminated against by his peers and even by some of the teachers."

Discrimination on the basis of caste is illegal under the Indian Constitution, and the government, through reverse discrimination laws, tries to make it possible for those of lower caste to improve their lives. There is a quota system, which reserves places in higher education and government employment for people from the 'scheduled castes'. These include *dalits* (those who were once untouchable), tribal people and 'other backward classes'. Some *dalits* have risen to high office in local governments. But I saw no evidence that the higher castes are prepared to take on traditionally low caste jobs.

While reverse discrimination may seem a laudable attempt to help those from the lower sections of society, not everyone is happy with the system. The Brahmin brothers running the hotel where I stayed in Jaisalmer had opened their *haveli* as a hotel because they felt that their own opportunities for employment were reduced.

Others complain that access to higher education and jobs should be based on merit, and that people from higher castes have been turned down in favour of less qualified members of the scheduled castes.

But it is not only people of high caste who discriminate against those of lower caste. An executive from the volunteer group's camp in Himachal Pradesh visited Lalsot and was taken to one of the farming villages where I taught.

"I was very offended," she exclaimed. "When we went to a house to meet the family of one of the children, they asked my caste. They would not invite me to sit down until they knew I was not lower in caste than themselves."

* * *

Giri had simplified his information about the caste system for me. It is an incredibly complex subject, and there are variations in practice between different groups of people and between the north and the south of the country. What Giri referred to as subcastes are *gotras*, which identify people through their lineage. In the north a person's *gotra* traces their direct patrilineal line of descent. Both men and women inherit their *gotra* from their father. But for some groups in the south descent is matrilineal, and one's *gotra* is that of one's mother.

"The maharaja could not pass on the title to any of his sons," my guide explained as I wandered round the palace in Kochi, in the southern state of Kerala. "When a maharaja died, the title passed to the eldest son of one of his sisters."

"What happened if he had no sisters, or none of them had sons?"

"One of his brothers, with the same mother as himself, could succeed. Otherwise succession would be through his maternal aunts."

Although the succession was through the female line, the maharaja was always a man.

Though in theory one's *gotra* is traced back through the generations, and can be authenticated by priests in Varanasi, this is not always possible in practice. Over hundreds of years the population has grown and changed, there have been influxes across borders or through trade, and direct lineal descent is not always easy to identify or prove.

In the countryside, groups of people following the same trade often lived together in the same village. Some still do today. The tiny village where I taught in the desert was named 'the village of the carpenters'. Most of the men in the village were carpenters, and the young wife I met there was married to a carpenter from another village. In the towns and cities there might be a weavers' quarter or a potters' quarter, and the untouchables would cluster together in a slum. For such a group of people, with the same trade or way of living, it was easier to take as their *gotra* the name of their local group or village.

The school near Lalsot was in a relatively large village, and many of the children I taught came from much smaller villages in the neighbourhood. I was given a list of all the children in my class and noticed that the family name recorded for each of them was the name of one of these little villages or of the village in which the school stood. So their *gotra* was the name of the village in which they lived.

* * *

> *B'ful, fair, well educated girl, from hi status family only, requ'd for h'some boy, 30, 5'10", IT eng., good salary, father ret'd Gov't servant.*

I was fascinated to read advertisements like this every Sunday in the weekly matrimonial supplement to the *Times of India*. There are two main sections: 'Wanted brides' and 'Wanted grooms'. The advertisements are arranged under subheadings denoting caste or family background, such as Brahmin, *Kshatriya*, *Yadav*, *Agrawal*, Sikh, Punjabi, Muslim, and occasionally Christian. A few advertisements say 'Caste no bar', though they are listed under a caste heading.

Of course, the readers of this English-language newspaper are educated and city based. Many of the families are looking for educated wives for their sons and may expect the girl to have a job or profession. Others want her to be 'homely'. Some parents advertise in the newspaper for a wife from home for a son working in America or Europe.

Often the advertisement gives the profession of the potential groom's father as well as his own qualifications, professional status and salary. Some give his date of birth, as astrology is important in deciding if a couple is suitably matched.

In the 'Wanted grooms' column the majority of women have good jobs, and the preferred profession of the required groom may be specified:

> *Well settled tall h'some boy reqd for c'vent educated b'ful slim girl, MBA wkg IT, from hi status fmly. Pref software eng/bank official.*

Attendance at a convent school implies that the girl has received an excellent education, but does not mean that she or her family are Christian. Often the boy must be 'well settled', and the minimum height or salary of potential applicants may be specified.

In all these advertisements most of the men are handsome, and the women are beautiful and sometimes slim as well. In this northern Indian edition of the paper, brides are often required to be fair, and both men and women may advertise themselves as fair-skinned.

"We in the north are Aryans, and our skin is much fairer than that of the Dravidians from the south," Giri had told me.

In the north at least, a pale skin seems to be a status symbol. Many face creams I saw in chemist shops claimed to whiten the skin.

* * *

The strict caste laws that determine a man's occupation also restrict marriage and may account for the relatively sudden end to the mixing between southern and northern Indian genes (mentioned in chapter 4). These laws only permit marriage between couples from the same caste. But things are much more complicated than that, as Giri explained to me.

"I may only marry within my own caste," he said, "but I may not marry within my own *gotra* (which I inherit from my father). Nor may I marry within the *gotra* of my mother or either of my grandmothers (which they inherited from their fathers)."

Restrictions such as these control marriage throughout the caste system, though not all are exactly the same in detail as those which Giri explained to me.

Clearly these rules must have been introduced to prevent incest and marriage between close relatives, which would be a risk for people obliged to marry within their own caste. But with the enormous increase in India's population, has the number of *gotras* grown in proportion? Do rules now ban marriage between people much more distantly related than first or second cousins? During my time in India the *Times of India* carried several reports of the murder of young couples by their families. Each couple was of the same caste but was related more closely than traditional marriage laws allowed. They had run away together, bringing shame to their families, and incurred a traditional punishment.

* * *

"You have big problems in the West, with so much divorce and a loss of family values," said my host in Jaipur. "It seems young people there are no longer caring for their parents when they get old."

This was the impression of Western society he had gleaned from the Indian newspapers.

"It's a result of allowing young people to choose their own partners," he continued. "They don't have the experience of life to choose wisely. Parents should arrange marriages for their children, and that makes for a much more stable family life. If the couple have problems they are not alone – it is the whole family's problem, and they are there to help sort it out."

Although he and his family were Christian, his own marriage had been an arranged one, and he and his wife had arranged the marriages of their son and daughter. From what I saw of his family life, his son and daughter-in-law's marriage was very happy and successful.

I wondered how much choice the young couple in an arranged marriage had.

"The girl can always refuse," one person told me.

"Did you know the girl your family were choosing for you?" I asked our driver in southern India.

"No, but my parents showed me photos of three different girls, and I picked the one I liked best."

He was very happy with his arranged marriage.

"I used to be a long-distance lorry driver, and I'd be away from home for a month or more," he told us. "But when I got married I wanted to spend more time with my wife. So now I drive tourist cars, and I'm not away for more than two weeks at a time."

Of course, his wife and baby were not left alone while he was away, since they lived with his parents on the family farm.

Traditionally bride and groom should not meet before the wedding and might never have seen one another before. There was a big wedding party at one of the hotels we stayed in on my original tour of India. The groom and his parents lived and worked in America, and the parents had arranged a marriage for their son to a girl from Rajasthan, from where they had emigrated. The girl had never travelled outside India, and bride and groom had not met before the ceremony. The bride was excited about going to live in America, but I could not help wondering how difficult and lonely she would find it, transported far from her family and friends to such a different culture.

But bride and groom are not always complete strangers before the wedding. One of my husband's graduate students from thirty years ago visited us with his wife.

"When I got a job in America my parents at home arranged a marriage for me," he told us. "She had professional qualifications but had not lived outside India before."

"How did you feel about it?" I asked his wife.

"Oh, I knew I would be able to get work in the US and, of course, though the marriage was arranged, we knew each other because we came from the same village."

With the advent of cheap mobile phones, things are changing. Even if they are forbidden to meet privately before the wedding, an engaged couple may be allowed to talk to one another by phone.

"I ring my fiancé every week, and we talk about what we will do and how we will live when we are married," one of the girls who worked in the kitchens of the volunteer camp told me.

* * *

Although many marriages are arranged, some young people do choose their own partners. A friend in Jaipur told me rather sadly:

"My son has just got divorced."

"Did you and your husband arrange the marriage?"

"No, he insisted on choosing for himself. Perhaps he will let us pick a wife for him next time."

Children may not always be able to refuse their parents, especially, I suspect, if they are women.

"I have fallen in love with someone," one young woman told me. "I just want to spend the rest of my life with him, but my mother will not allow me to marry him."

"Is he from a higher or lower caste than you?"

"No, we are the same level, but I am not permitted to marry him," she said sadly.

* * *

Although I did not meet Hitesh again after my visit to Udaipur, we kept in touch by phone and email. He did well in his German course and was recruited by Amazon to work in Chennai, communicating with their German suppliers. He had hoped that his family would be pleased that he had a good job. But they were upset that he had moved so far away from home, to a state where he did not know the language and that seemed to his parents as foreign as another country.

However, he was able to see his girlfriend, who was in India for six months as part of her course. Later, after she graduated, she got a job in Delhi. Later still Hitesh had great news for me. His family had held a family conclave, with his uncles and aunts and cousins as well as his parents and siblings. They decided that if they arranged a marriage for him and he was unhappy in it, then they would be unhappy too. So they would accept his girlfriend as a future member of the family, and Hitesh was able to take her to meet them all. They were working in cities thousands of kilometres apart and could only see each other occasionally, but at least now Hitesh's family no longer opposed his choice of partner.

* * *

I had met a huge variety of people, from the children and their families in the villages where I taught, to the Maharaja and his wife. A board on the wall in the headmaster's study in the school near Lalsot listed the teachers, with their names and qualifications. Most of their family names were ones I recognised as relatively high caste compared to the *gotras* of the children, which were names of local farming villages. The tailor and the families of the girls in my Computing and English class in Shiv must also have been more prosperous and of higher caste than the children in my village schools. The lowest caste people I had encountered so far were the Snake Charmers.

The Indians I met working for the volunteer organisation came from a range of backgrounds. Although some were from high caste families, others belonged to lower castes. But all the executives were from backgrounds prosperous enough to have provided them with a higher education. In the volunteer camps there was no caste-based discrimination, and everyone joined in the volleyball games before supper and in celebrating a birthday or Holi.

In the villages where I had worked the people, though poor, were not *dalits*. I had seen people living on the streets in Delhi, and looked down from the plane on the slums of Mumbai. But I had not worked with street or slum children. That was to change on my fourth volunteer placement when I went to Kolkata.

Chapter 7

LEARNING HINDI IN JAIPUR

The ground was shrouded in a sandy haze as I gazed out of the window on the short flight from Delhi to Jaipur. I was met by sun and warmth, and Rajesh from the volunteer organisation, who was welcoming and chatty and led me to the minibus where I recognised the driver as one that I had met the previous year.

When we arrived at Mr A's house his grandson Vaishant was waiting to greet me, peeping out through the foliage at the front. He led me up the iron staircase to the flat roof, while Rajesh followed with my luggage. My room opened onto the roof. It was bright and cheerful, with white walls and orange and red coverings on the bed and the cushions of two chairs. Mr A came up to greet me, and we sat and talked for a while. I was tired after the flight from Europe, followed by too little sleep before flying on to Jaipur.

"You should rest now," he suggested. "Come down for *chai* later in the afternoon when you wake."

So I lay on my bed luxuriating in the warmth, both of my welcome and the weather, and soon drifted off to sleep.

On this, my fourth trip to India, and third as a volunteer, I was to experience life in a middle-class Indian home, living with a host family for four weeks while I took Hindi lessons. The household consisted of Mr A, his son Deepak, daughter-in-law Veena, and their son Vaishant. I had spent three nights with them, in the company of three other volunteers, during our inaugural week in Jaipur the previous year.

Mr A was in his seventies. His wife had died a few years before, and he missed her very much. But he had found a new interest in life when the volunteer organisation approached him and asked him to host volunteers.

"I asked them what accommodation was needed," he said, "and we built the two rooms and the bathroom on the flat roof. I have enjoyed meeting young people from all over the world."

The house was in the middle of an area of small dusty streets sandwiched between two main roads. Deepak and Veena sold sweets, biscuits, water, milk and ice cream, and topped up mobile phones, from a little single-storey shop next door to the main building. Beyond that was an empty lot that I looked down on from the flat roof, where people dumped rubbish. Occasionally someone would set fire to it, and Mr A told me that when it got too full the local council would send a bulldozer to take the refuse away and dump it somewhere else. A skinny sandy-brown bitch and her puppy, their thin tails curled over their backs, lived and scavenged in the rubbish. It was a quiet area, and I heard little of the traffic on the main roads not far away.

Walking down the street past the tip I passed a double row of ice cream vendors' bicycles, parked outside a yard. Each carried a sunshade, painted in blue and white stripes below a band of bright yellow. A refrigerated box in front for the ices, similarly decorated, bore the inscription 'Mother Dairy'.

"Mother Dairy is a very big government co-op. It is the only dairy supplying milk, *ghee* and cheese to a large region around

Jaipur – including places as far away as Dausa and Lalsot," Mr A told me.

The street ended in a T-junction with another narrow road. Two dark brown cows with curving horns were always tethered in the shade of a *neem* tree in a courtyard beside one of the houses just down to the right. But I usually turned left towards the volunteer headquarters – only a few minutes' walk from home.

* * *

In the mornings I woke to the cries of the street vendor wheeling his barrow laden with brightly coloured fruit and vegetables, and the loud piercing call of a tiny green tailorbird hidden in the leaves of the trees and creepers which shaded the front of the house. A neighbour would be doing his morning *puja* on his balcony, hands raised in prayer towards the rising sun. At this time of day the air was pleasantly fresh, and I sat outside my room beside a row of potted plants with pink and white daisy-like flowers, to prepare my lessons or finish my homework before breakfast.

The family were up as soon as it was light, to get chores done while the air was still cool. Then we breakfasted shortly before nine. Veena cooked an Indian breakfast – some days rice flakes with onion, peanuts, chilli and peppers, on others a wheat porridge. On special occasions she made bread rolls stuffed with a savoury mixture of potato, onion and chilli, and of course there was always *chai*. She was an excellent cook and produced a variety of delicious meals from her tiny kitchen at the side of the dining area in the main room of the house. She did not speak much English, so I could not have proper conversations with her, but she was always smiling and cheerful.

Around six o'clock every afternoon Veena made *chai*, and I would sit with Mr A, sipping the hot sweet tea spiced with cardamom, in the big living room which stretched across the whole front of the house. We sat in comfortable chairs, with a coffee table in front of us. Other easy chairs lined the walls, and there was a computer on a table at one side from which I could send emails. The room was cooled by ceiling fans and shaded by the foliage of the bushes and flowering climbers that Mr A had planted outside. He watered them every day. Opposite the front door the narrower dining area opened off the living room, with the kitchen to its left. Against the back wall stood a big refrigerator, and beside it a wash basin – that essential feature of all Indian eating areas.

Veena provided me with bottles of water from a purifier in the kitchen every day. They were put to cool in the fridge, but Mr A warned me not to drink the water immediately.

"It is bad for you to drink ice-cold water. Let it warm up in your room for a while."

As we drank our *chai* Mr A and I chatted about many things.

"We are from Ajmer, where the Scottish missionaries were based," he explained. "They arrived in the middle of the nineteenth century. There were disastrous droughts around that time, and the missionaries organised famine relief. They set up schools, too, and provided medical care. So they were a great help to the community, and the people welcomed them. My family converted to Christianity at that time. When they were children my sister and youngest brother played with the son and daughter of the missionary. They were about the same age. The missionary's son could be a bit naughty and would get them all into trouble."

"Did you learn English from the missionaries?"

"No. I was taught English in school, and then I improved it by reading religious texts in English."

His wife had taught at a college, and they were unable to live together in the same town for some years after their marriage.

"At last I got a job in Jaipur, and we built this house. When we first arrived there were only four Christian families here, but now there are thirty or forty."

Mr A took a great interest in the volunteers who stayed in his house, many of them school leavers or in their early twenties.

"One of the young volunteers was very upset. She was teaching children in the slums here," he told me one day. "She felt that she was doing so little for them and that they needed so much. I tried to reassure her. You can't change their lives in only a few weeks, but it is important to help them get an education, and each small contribution is worthwhile."

He was a father figure to her, and she kept in touch by email after she had returned home.

Mr A was an accountant and had had an important position in the Rajasthani local government in Jaipur. He was very cynical about people in general.

"That company that sends you out here – they charge you a lot of money, don't they?"

"EIL is a not-for-profit organisation. They have to take something to cover their costs, but most of what I pay is for my expenses here and to maintain the work of the volunteer organisation."

"Don't you believe it. Everyone is out to make money for himself. If anyone offers to do something for you, you should realise that they will expect payment."

There is a lot of bribery and corruption at all levels in India. Hitesh had told me that one of his college friends now had a good job as a tourist guide in Delhi.

"If he can get employment like that in Delhi, maybe you will be able to as well," I suggested.

"No, I wouldn't be able to afford it. He had to give the guy who got him the job a new car."

But, as a Christian, Mr A refused to take bribes.

"Other people in the government offices would ask for things before they would do anything for anyone. But I became known for never demanding a bribe. My brothers are the same. I am the oldest, and I helped my four younger brothers get good jobs. One is a doctor, another a civil engineer, another was managing director of a bank and has just retired, and another works for the railway company."

Not only did Mr A refuse bribes, he uncovered illicit dealings and exposed the perpetrators.

"I uncovered a scam involving fraudulent army pensions," he told me. "Then there were the elderly widows from Sind. They had crossed the border into India at partition. But there was a shopkeeper who organised a scam and was defrauding the widows of their pensions. The women came to me for help, and I managed to expose the shopkeeper and get them their pensions."

Mr A, Vaishant and I ate breakfast and dinner together every day, and his grandfather encouraged Vaishant to say grace in English before the meal. Veena and Deepak could not leave the shop unattended, and Veena often took her meal after we had eaten, before relieving her husband in the shop. I learned to eat with my fingers, Indian style. But if some dish defeated me there were always spoons available on the table. I did not have to get used to very hot curries as less chilli is used in the north than in the south of the country.

* * *

Every weekday morning, and sometimes on Saturdays as well, I spent three hours learning Hindi with Subhadra. I had kept in touch with her since our first meeting, when I had stayed in her house with Lena and Tina on my first trip as a volunteer. This year I was at last fulfilling my long-held dream to take Hindi lessons.

We sat at a long table in a basement room in the volunteer headquarters, kept cool by two big fans hanging from the ceiling. Subhadra had decorated the walls with colourful posters of vegetables and fruit, animals, plants and people. There was a whiteboard on one wall, on which I attempted to write Hindi words at Subhadra's dictation. This was not easy. Hindi is an Indo-European language, and the grammar is reminiscent of Latin, which I learnt at school. But it is difficult for a European to pronounce, and worse still to hear, the subtle differences between the four different 't' and 'd' consonants used in all the languages of the Indian sub-continent.

During the first week Subhadra coached me in the pronunciation of the letters in the Devanagari alphabet, which I had learnt to read from my *Teach yourself Hindi* book. Many of the consonants have an aspirated form (where you breathe out as you pronounce it) as well as an un-aspirated form, and the two are represented by different letters. But for the 't' sound, and similarly for 'd', there are four different letters, corresponding to two ways of pronouncing each of the aspirated and un-aspirated consonants. For one you must place the tip of your tongue against your teeth as you say it (the dental form), while for the other the tip of your tongue must curl back to touch the ridge behind your top teeth as you pronounce the 't' or 'd' (the retroflex form). For someone like me, who has not heard the language spoken from early childhood, it is almost impossible to hear the slight but important difference between dental and retroflex consonants.

I discovered that in speaking English I place the tip of my tongue at the top of my teeth, just touching the ridge behind them, as I pronounce a word with a 't' or a 'd' in it, so that I produce a sound somewhere between the two Indian forms. Indians transcribe our 't' and 'd' as retroflex sounds in words they have taken from English, such as 'tomato' or 'doctor'.

Using a dental instead of a retroflex consonant in Hindi changes the meaning of a word completely. I realised for the first time that when I had taught the children in school about hundreds, tens and units I might have been misleading them completely. The word for 'tens' starts with a dental 'd' followed by an 'h'. (This is not quite the same as an aspirated dental 'd' as it has a slight gap between the 'd' and the aspirate.) On the other hand the almost identical word starting with a retroflex aspirated 'd' means 'two and a half'.

Although I had difficulties with pronunciation, I found Hindi words that reminded me of similar words in European languages, and this made learning the language somewhat easier than I had feared. All the question words, meaning 'what', 'why', 'who', 'where', and so on start with a 'k' sound, as they do in French, and the numbers one to ten have a familiar ring to them. Some of the verbs were easy to remember – *suna*, meaning to hear, and *dena*, to give, reminded me of sound and donate.

Some Hindi words have crept into English. For example, the phrase 'take a dekko' comes from the Hindi for 'look', and 'pukka' (used by Jamie Oliver in his television cookery series) is a Hindi word meaning 'ripe'. Many English words have been adopted into Hindi, like 'doctor' and 'tomato' which I mentioned earlier. But there were some surprises.

"Is *brinjal* the Hindi for aubergine?" I asked Subhadra.

She was surprised.

"Oh no – that's an English word. The Hindi is *baingan*."

Another time, as I read from the Hindi, I came across a word I could not translate.

"That means a godown."

"But what is that? What does it mean?"

"You must know that – it's English. It's a place for storing things."

Later I found both godown and *brinjal* in the Oxford English Dictionary, identified as Anglo-Indian words dating from the sixteenth and seventeenth centuries respectively.

* * *

I was always brought *chai* at the beginning of my lesson by Rinku, whom I had first met in Shiv. She was working in the kitchen here in Jaipur now and would come to chat with me after my lesson, when I went up to the roof for lunch. I was the only volunteer in Jaipur for most of my stay, and so the others eating there were the Indian staff. They had usually finished when I arrived, but I chatted with a couple of the drivers who came in later, and tried to say a few sentences in my newly learned Hindi.

I found that when listening to my host family talking I could begin to hear it as a string of words, a few of which I recognised, rather than as an indecipherable babble. But the cook had a strong local accent, and I found her very difficult to understand. Some of the staff were very good at helping me by speaking slowly, but when I replied they were inclined to finish my sentences for me because I was so slow. One of my difficulties was that the verb comes at the end of a sentence or phrase, as in German.

Hindi is usually spoken as a mother tongue only in a relatively small region near Delhi. I think some of my difficulty in understanding what people said to me was that Hindi was their second language, and their accents differed depending on where they came from. When one of the executives gave me a lift one day I asked him in Hindi if he was going home to his village. He and his companion roared with laughter.

"You are speaking pure Hindi," he said. "We never do. We always talk in a mixture of Hindi and our own language, with some English thrown in as well."

One day a little five-year-old girl came to sit by me while I ate. I asked her name and age in Hindi, without getting any reply, but she showed me a book with pictures of animals, fruit and vegetables, and so on, labelled with their English names. I tried to get her to say the words in Hindi, but again with no success.

"She doesn't speak Hindi," the cook told me. "Her mother has come here to work in the kitchen, but they are from West Bengal, so the child only speaks Bengali."

When the cook's young nephew was on holiday he joined me and the little girl. He understood my Hindi sufficiently well to tell me his name and that he too was five years old.

* * *

When Vaishant came home from school in the afternoon he often came up to talk to me as I sat doing my homework. Sometimes he helped me by translating a Hindi word I did not know.

"I have to do dictation in Hindi too," he told me when I told him what I did in my lessons.

He attended a private school where teaching was through English, and though he spoke Hindi at home he had to learn to write it.

"He is not very good at writing in Hindi," his grandfather said. "He needs to work at it."

But Vaishant was good at writing in English, and one day when I needed to concentrate on my homework I gave him a sheet of paper and suggested he should write a little story in English. He brought me back a page about his school day, written in beautiful copperplate handwriting.

The school he attended had been set up by Catholic missionaries and was now run by Indian Catholics, many of them from the south of India.

"We sent him to a local school at first," Mr A said, "but the educational standards were not good enough. This school is a much better one."

One day Vaishant showed me his textbooks for the new school year, which would start at the beginning of April.

"These are for my new class," he said. "I'll have lessons in English, Hindi and Maths, and this book is for Social Studies, and that one for Ecological Living. We have Computers too, but the one I like best is Science because we make things."

"What about Geography?"

"We have a book about India and what people do," he replied.

I was impressed that these children in the nine to ten age group were being taught about social and ecological matters. I liked the look of the textbooks, in particular the English one, which included excerpts from books such as Paul Gallico's *The Snow Goose*, C S Lewis's *The Lion, the Witch and the Wardrobe*, and *David Copperfield*. There were real poems too, so much better, to my mind, than the rather trivial pieces written especially for Irish primary school children.

Vaishant was asthmatic, and his family worried about his health. On a hot afternoon I bought myself an ice cream in the shop and asked if I could get one for Vaishant too. But his mother said:

"No, it's not good for his cough."

One day when he came to talk to me he had a small packet on a string round his neck under his shirt.

"It has a smell to help protect me from infection," he explained. "We are all wearing them at school this week because people are getting sick."

Another week he had a different packet round his neck, containing a magnet.

At mealtimes his grandfather always tried to make Vaishant eat more chapatis so that he would put on weight – he was a slight child, though not skinny.

Sometimes Vaishant brought his toy cars to show me, or games to play with me. Two which he enjoyed were Scrabble-like games, in which we competed at spelling English words. He also had me playing badminton on the flat roof, or rolling a ball to knock down a little pile of stones. One day, perhaps inspired by a science lesson, he wanted to boil water in a bowl made from a coconut shell over a fire in a tin can. He had put leaves and small twigs in the bottom of the can, but each time he lit them they went out.

"The fire needs air to burn," I told him. "It goes out because there is no way for new air to get in once it has used what's in the can."

He wanted to try again with a hole for air at the bottom of the can, but his mother put a stop to this game.

"She says it is making too much smoke and it is bad for me," he said.

One afternoon Vaishant changed out of his school uniform and took me to a playground not far away. We walked down a dusty street and turned left past the cricket stadium – from my flat roof I would hear the roars and cheers of the crowd each time there was a big match there – then turned down another small road lined with houses and came to a little park enclosed by low walls. The grass was thin, with patches of bare sandy earth. Some bigger boys were playing cricket with two bats and a ball but no stumps. At one end was a tiny temple, and a group of men in white sat on the ground nearby, deep in conversation and a card game.

The swings had been vandalised, but Vaishant climbed and swung on their empty frames. Several small children were enjoying themselves on a slide. An elderly woman who was with them smiled at me and patted the ground beside her, inviting me to sit with her, but Vaishant was too shy to join the others.

"Time me while I run all round the park," he said.

He got three-quarters of the way round before he gave up and we turned for home and dinner.

* * *

It was Vaishant's ninth birthday, and Veena's brother had brought his two children and his mother to visit for the weekend. The little girl was almost a year older than Vaishant, and the boy a couple of years younger. At breakfast Deepak brought out a chocolate cake decorated with lots of creamy icing and one candle, which relit itself so that Vaishant had to blow it out several times. We all ate a slice and wished Vaishant a happy birthday.

The three children came up to the flat roof and asked me to play ball games with them. But I gave up after a short while, as it was too hot for me to run around in the midday sun. The little girl came to sit by me in the shade.

"What's your name?" I asked.

"At home I am called Gun-gun, but that's not my school name."

Her English was good, and she stayed to chat and ask me about my Hindi lessons. She helped by translating one or two sentences that I couldn't understand. Later Mr A told me:

"She said you wrote very nicely in Hindi as well as English. She could not understand why you should want to learn Hindi. She asked me if it was a language you spoke at home in Ireland."

Later that afternoon, when it was cooler, I was invited to join the children and their fathers on a trip to the zoo. I had decided to concentrate on my Hindi during these four weeks and had avoided visits to the city centre and the tourist attractions. So this outing was a treat for me as well as the children.

We set off in the uncle's car. It was exhilarating to drive through the chaotic traffic, with the image of Jesus and the Sacred Heart bobbing below the rear-view mirror where a Hindu family would have hung Ganesh. Close to the ornate turreted museum building we found a parking space, on the opposite side of the road from the zoo. The children took our hands as we stood at the roadside trying to find a gap in the roaring traffic. Even on the pedestrian crossing the cars, *tuk-tuks* and scooters would not stop for us but just hooted at us to get out of their way. Deepak laughed and said:

"Indian traffic has no order."

Outside the gates of the zoo the colourful crowd was being offered cold drinks, ice creams and trinkets at little stalls. Once inside the two little boys rushed round, climbing on fences wherever possible, while Gun-gun stayed by my side and chatted to me in English, and the fathers stood back and talked together.

The animals were mostly hidden in what shade they could find at the backs of their cages, but the alligators were sunning themselves beside their pool. I felt sorry for the tiger and other large animals in their small concrete prisons. But I enjoyed wandering through the grounds, which were bright with flowering trees, and watching the kites soaring lazily overhead in a cloudless sky. Gun-gun told me she really liked the birds best. So when we had exhausted the zoo we crossed the road to the aviary and admired the parakeets, hornbills, owls and vultures.

Another hectic drive through throngs of cars, *tuk-tuks*, taxis and mopeds brought us to the cool and quiet of home. Gun-gun reported that I had acted as their grandmother at the zoo, which earned me a beaming smile from her *dadi-ji*.

The visitors left in mid afternoon the next day, and the children and their *dadi* embraced me.

* * *

A deep magenta bougainvillea wreathed the iron railings by the steps at the front of the house, and one of the small trees was covered in bright yellow flowers, from which tiny purple sunbirds sipped nectar. Cactus plants in pots were a riot of pink and yellow flowers, and a little lizard sunned itself beside them.

I loved to watch the birds that visited my flat roof. The pair of tiny tailor birds were there every day, and sparrows were building nests in crevices in the back wall. Doves flew down, and common mynahs perched on the rooftop next door. Sometimes I saw a pair of colourful Brahminy mynas there. They were much smarter than the common mynahs, with orange chests and underparts, grey wings and black heads and tails. Once I heard the lovely bubbly song of bulbuls and looked out to see a couple of red-vented ones, with a scarlet patch beneath the tail which gives them their name.

Beyond the edge of the flat roof was a pole festooned with electrical wires, on which stripy squirrels ran back and forth. A black box with electrical connections inside was attached to the pole at roof level, and there was often a squirrel sitting on top. One day I saw a squirrel's tail hanging out through a hole in the bottom of the box. It looked as though the squirrels were risking electrocution to use the box as a nest.

One bird fanned out its tail like a mynah, but its plumage was pale fawn rather than dark, and it had no yellow flash under its eye. I could not identify it until Vaishant was with me one day, and I asked him what it was.

"That is a bird's child," he said, and I realised it was a young mynah which had not yet got its adult colouring.

One morning as I was sitting working, the sparrows set up a great clamour, and when I looked around there was a big male macaque monkey on the roof above me. He sat and surveyed the scene for a while before making his way round the walls above me, to the roof of the neighbouring house and then across the road to the roof opposite. The dog that lived next door started to whine and make a fuss, but when its owner came to find out what was wrong he could not see the monkey because it was above him. Soon other monkeys followed. A mother with a baby sat above me while the little one jumped and played around. Then it climbed on its mother's back, and they followed the others round the walls.

Mr A came up with a stick, to chase off any monkeys that might remain to play havoc with his plants.

"They pick the yellow flowers off my tree," he told me. "They are a real nuisance. Once we left the house door open and a monkey came in. It went straight to the fridge at the back of the room, opened it, took out a papaya and ran off with it."

"They take clothes left out to dry too," Vaishant said. "A monkey pulled all the buttons off one of my shirts."

As I watched, one monkey helped himself to a bright yellow and red piece of clothing from the washing line on the roof opposite and draped it over the wall next to him while he sat and ate something he had found there. It was almost half an hour before the monkey troupe moved out of sight.

* * *

I was to go to a wedding in Palampur after leaving Jaipur, and Subhadra offered to take me to buy a sari to wear. So one Saturday morning we set off in her car. Although she had learnt to drive in London she had acquired Indian driving habits. Coming out of her road onto a larger one we needed to turn right. But the barrier down the middle of the main road prevented her crossing to the appropriate lane. Instead of turning left to go round the end of the barrier she turned right and drove against the flow of traffic till there was a gap in the barrier where she could move into the correct lane.

First of all we stopped at a shop to drop off her cotton quilts, which are used like duvets in the winter.

"They need cleaning," she explained, "and then they will top them up with new cotton filling."

On the pavement outside the shop was a big scales, and the quilts were weighed.

"When I collect them they will be weighed again to show how much cotton has been added," she said.

"You always look so smart, Subhadra," I told her. "Where do you get your clothes? I feel mine all look a bit cheap and dowdy."

"There's a good dress shop close by. Let's go and see if there is something you would like there."

In the shop I selected a couple of *salwar kameez* to try on. Subhadra found a *kameez* in bright turquoise, trimmed with white and spangled with silver sequins. It was to be worn with white trousers, with tight legs that wrinkled slightly above the ankles, and a white scarf.

"Try this one. It will suit you."

I thought it looked a bit too garish, but when I tried it on I found she was right, and I fell for it. Although this was a smart shop, for relatively affluent Indian ladies, I paid no more than I had paid for my other outfits in the shops frequented by volunteers.

Then we went to a sari shop. We entered a long narrow room with raised mattresses all along each side and bales of brightly coloured sari lengths stacked on the shelves which covered all the walls from floor to ceiling. Several men were sitting cross-legged on the mattress at the left, waiting for customers. One of them rose and offered us chairs facing the mattress on the right.

While he pulled down a selection of sari lengths another man brought us each a glass of water. Subhadra explained in Hindi what I was looking for. She said I must have silk because polyester would be too slippery. But he had no pure silk in stock because it was the end of winter, and silk is considered too hot for summer. He brought out a length of material which Subhadra examined carefully. Then she turned to me.

"This is artificial silk. I think that would be best. What sort of colours do you want?"

"No reds, oranges or yellows. They don't suit me."

When she relayed this to the shopkeeper he pulled out several lengths in greens and blues with geometric patterns in contrasting colours, but Subhadra and I felt they were not quite right for a wedding. Then he produced a magnificent dusky pink sari with a pattern of tiny flowers in gold thread. Subhadra asked what other colours he had, and he showed us some with the same gold pattern in half a dozen different shades. I chose an apple green and a deep peacock blue one to try, as well as the pink.

We were ushered into the next room – another long narrow room with a raised mattress down the right-hand side and mirrors covering the walls on the left and at the end. I took off my shoes and climbed onto the mattress, and the shopkeeper proceeded to pleat the material in the appropriate place along its length. Then he started wrapping it round me (on top of my clothes), and when he came to the pleats, which have to be in centre front, he secured it all with an elastic belt. The remaining length of material came under my right arm, across my chest and over my left shoulder, falling almost to my knees behind.

I tried all three colours.

"I think the peacock blue suits you best," decided Subhadra.

The shopkeeper agreed with her, and after surveying myself in the mirrors from all angles so did I.

So I was unwound, and we went back to the main shop. There he cut off the end section of the cloth, which was for making a matching blouse.

"They don't make up the blouses here, or sell the underskirts," Subhadra explained. "We'll go elsewhere for that."

The shopkeeper kept the remaining six-metre length and would hem the ends of the sari. The cost of this magnificent piece of material was just under twenty euro.

"I can collect it for you next week," Subhadra said.

Next we went to the underskirt shop. This was a little way away, in the market. Again it was a narrow shop, with floor-to-ceiling shelves stacked with underskirts of every imaginable shade. It was easy to find one to match the peacock of my sari.

Finally we visited the tailor, in a tiny hut very close to where I lived. There I was measured and had to decide how short the sleeves should be. Did I want a round or square neck? How low in front? How low at the back? He measured my length from the waist and the length of the underskirt and said it needed to have one inch taken off. So I left the underskirt with him, as well as the material for the blouse, and was told to collect them on Monday.

* * *

By the beginning of April the temperature was forty degrees in the middle of the day. There was no longer any need for the water to be heated for my bucket showers. In the morning it was lukewarm in the tap, and really hot by the afternoon, because the cold water tank was on the bathroom roof.

Vaishant's new school year started, after only a few days' holiday. He changed to his summer uniform of navy shorts and a white open-necked shirt with short sleeves – in the winter he wore long grey trousers with a long-sleeved white shirt and blue and yellow striped tie. His classes now started early, at seven in the morning, and finished just after one, so that the children would be at home during the hot afternoon.

"When do you get a longer holiday?" I asked him.

"Our longest one is coming soon. It starts in the middle of May and ends in July when the monsoon comes."

As the days grew hotter the frangipani tree produced buds, but I left before they opened into perfumed white flowers. After dark I sat out under the stars, bathed in the fragrance of gardenia flowers which gleamed white against dark foliage at the edge of the roof. Vaishant made me a garland of them, and his mother pinned it in my hair.

I found that forty degrees in the city was less bearable than in the countryside at Shiv or Lalsot. Hemmed in by tall buildings the air is less fresh. I kept the fan on all night and left my door open, just closing over the outer mesh door to keep out insects, though there were not many mosquitos yet.

"They will come up from the south in June, just before the monsoon," Mr A told me.

Veena filled my water bottle from an earthenware pot on a stand, kept cool by condensation. But the walls of my room were warm to the touch, and my bottle of water was soon lukewarm. It was only a couple of days before I left Jaipur that I discovered how to keep it cool – I placed it in the sink in my room, with a damp facecloth wrapped round it, and that worked perfectly.

One of the family's relations was celebrating a sixtieth birthday with a prayer meeting followed by a dinner. Veena appeared in a beautiful cornflower blue sari trimmed with gold, and Vaishant looked like a little maharaja in a shining turquoise tunic delicately patterned in white, with white trousers and a white sash over one shoulder. Deepak just wore smart Western trousers and a shirt. All three of them climbed onto the moped and set off.

"I can't go out to things like that anymore," said Mr A. "It is too far to walk. In any case, I find now that eating rich meals late in the evening is not good for me."

* * *

"Happy Easter," we said to each other on Easter morning. Veena and Deepak had been to church at five o'clock in the morning. That was a long service lasting three hours. There was another, an hour long, at half past eight.

Now I had only two more days before leaving for Palampur in Himachal Pradesh. It would be my first visit to the mountains, and I was excited, though I was sorry to be leaving my host family and Subhadra.

I had my final Hindi lesson with Subhadra at her house. She had turned a little room next to the main house into a teaching room. It was cool and airy, and we looked out onto her small garden. She grew bonsai trees in pots. A miniature bougainvillea, less than a foot high, was covered with pale pink blossoms.

"I have to prune them every two weeks," she told me, "and then every two years I prune their roots."

On my last evening Veena prepared a special dinner for me – vegetable biryani, little balls made from gram (chickpea) flour in a delicately spiced sauce, potato cooked with aubergine, raita (cucumber in yogurt) and chapatis. Indians do not usually have a dessert, though Veena often sent me up a little dish of fresh fruit in the afternoon. This evening she produced a fruit custard, filled with pieces of apple, banana and grapes.

The next morning I brought my sari round to Subhadra's house for a lesson in putting it on. I found it hard to get the pleats right and harder still to pin it at the shoulder. She gave me some long safety pins for that, a set of *bindis*, and a lovely piece of material in soft turquoise patterned with white.

"Get it made up into a *salwar kameez* when you reach Palampur," she said.

Then she showed me how to make chapatis, placing the thin discs of dough directly onto the gas ring, and we had lunch – mung dal, potatoes and peas in a hot sauce, spinach in curd (yogurt), a bean sprout salad, and the chapatis she had made. She produced a dessert too. It was made from ground rice, cooked with spices and then chilled, and decorated with little pieces of candy and nuts.

Subhadra had taught me a lot in four weeks, though my conversational abilities were still very limited. I needed to work out what I wanted to say in advance and found it hard to understand what people said to me unless they spoke very slowly. She had been very kind, and I was sad to say goodbye.

I stopped off at the volunteer headquarters on my way home, to say my goodbyes to the staff there. I stocked up with bottles of water from the shop, Vaishant helped me bring down my luggage, and it was time to say farewell to the family. I had so much enjoyed my stay with them, and they had made me feel a part of the family. But we promised to keep in touch with one another by email. Then the minibus arrived to take me to the station and the overnight train to the foothills of the Himalayas.

* * *

I love overnight train journeys in India. The long carriages have compartments which can be curtained off from the corridor. Each has a set of three bunks on either side, one above another, and there is a pair of tiered bunks on the opposite side of the corridor lying parallel to the direction of travel. The '3-tier AC' carriages have glass windows and air conditioning, and the blast of cold air when I got in was often a shock. The three-tier carriages without air conditioning have open, barred windows, allowing in fresh air. In the winter in Rajasthan I never found travelling that way too hot.

As daylight fades the *khana walla* comes along crying his wares, and sells rice, curries and chapatis for the evening meal. Evening turns to night, and all the upper bunks are pulled down. The travellers make up their beds with the sheets, pillows and blankets which are provided. Indians are adept at tucking the sheets in so that they are still in place the next morning, but I usually found that mine came adrift and wrapped themselves round me.

"*Chai, chai, chai.*"

The call of the *chai walla* wakes me in the morning, as he comes through the carriage with a kettle of hot *chai* which he pours into paper cups. When Lena and I were returning to Delhi from Shiv we saw a tiny mouse finishing the drops of *chai* left in a cup under the bunk on the opposite side of the corridor.

I had travelled overnight by train from Jaipur to Barmer, Barmer to Delhi, and Dausa to Udaipur and back, but on each of those occasions I was with other volunteers. This time I was travelling alone, though my driver had found me my seat in 3-tier AC carriage B1 when the 'Aii Jat express' arrived from Ajmer. It was the first time I had boarded an Indian train which was on time.

From my window seat I watched the life of the countryside flit past – parched sandy earth with the occasional bright green irrigated fields, little farm houses with cows and water buffalo tethered outside, goats and sheep herded by patient men or children, women in saris carrying water pots or bundles on their heads. At level crossings the road on either side was packed with cars, tractors and mopeds. They spread right across its width on both sides of the track, so that I wondered how the traffic would manage to sort itself out and allow passage of vehicles travelling in opposite directions over the crossing when the train had passed.

I shared my compartment with two women and a horde of little children. The women chattered to one another continuously, and their menfolk looked in occasionally from further down the carriage. One little boy plucked up the courage to ask, in hesitant English:

"Where you go?"

"Chakki Bank."

"Where you sleep?"

"Here – *yahan*."

The women bought food from the *khana walla* and fed the children. The volunteer company had provided me with a supper of potatoes cooked with cumin seeds, and an orange, but I was not very hungry after the farewell lunch I had eaten with Subhadra.

As it grew dark the husbands came and collected the women and children, and two businessmen replaced them. I was not sure if the families were going to leave the train at the next stop, or whether some people from the husbands' compartment had left the train and they had negotiated an exchange with the remaining two men. Whatever the reason, my original companions left, and the businessmen sat silently working on their laptops.

I was tired, and as it grew dark I quickly fell asleep in the air-conditioned carriage, without making up my bed. I woke around midnight when the train stopped at Delhi, and talked to a woman and her cousin who joined me and the businessmen in the compartment.

"I am going to Chakki Bank, and I'll be picked up from there to drive to Palampur," I told her in answer to her query.

"Chakki Bank is in the Punjab, on the border with Himachal Pradesh," she said. "We are going to Jammu, two stops further on. We have a family wedding there. My husband and children can't leave during the week, but they will join us at the weekend."

Jammu is the part of Kashmir which is mainly Hindu.

"You speak English very well," I told her. She spoke it perfectly, with very little accent.

"I am a schoolteacher – I teach English to fourteen-year-olds."

We exchanged information about our families.

"I have two daughters. The older one has just had her twenty-first birthday."

"You don't look old enough to have a child that age."

"I got married very young. We lived in Kashmir, but my family fled in the 1980s, because of the violence and incursions from Pakistan. Now I live in Delhi with my husband and the girls."

Her cousin helped me make up my bed, but I was warm, and I soon dropped off to sleep with only the sheet over me. Much later I woke briefly to find my companion covering me with the blanket.

"It is getting very cold now; you'll need the cover," she said.

When I woke again and pulled aside the blind to look out it was five o'clock in the morning and still dark. The train was stopped at a station, and there were bright flashes of white light on the horizon. I wondered briefly if it was the light of gunfire on the border, but suddenly it began to teem with rain and I realised it was lightning.

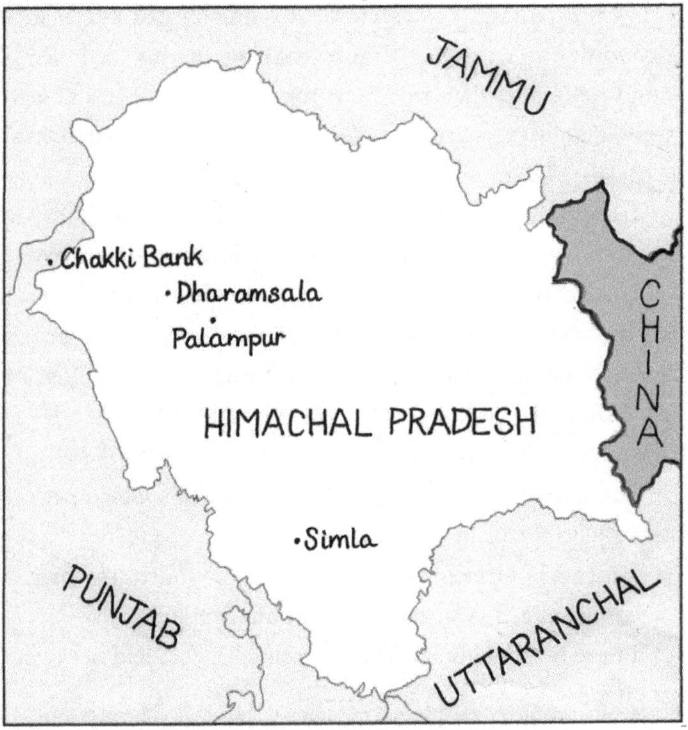

Map of Himachal Pradesh

It seemed that the train was at least an hour late, as there should have been no stop between four in the morning and my own stop around six. My friend from the night before woke, and I asked her how I would know when we were reaching Chakki Bank.

"The carriage attendant is sleeping just next to the exit door of the carriage. Go and wake him and ask how late we are and when we will get there."

I went down to the area at the end of the carriage, and there a figure lay on a trolley, shrouded from head to toe in a white sheet. I finally plucked up the courage to say tentatively:

"Excuse me."

The figure unwrapped its head, and I asked when we would reach my destination.

"We will be there at seven minutes after seven," he said, and covered himself up again.

So I used the rather unsavoury washroom and returned to my compartment. Soon the *chai walla* came round, and everyone began to wake up. The world outside was green and damp – a complete contrast to Rajasthan. Just after seven the carriage attendant came along to tell me we would be arriving in a few minutes. I said goodbye to my travelling companions and stepped out onto a very wet platform.

Chapter 8

VOLUNTEERING IN HIMACHAL PRADESH

Sunil, one of the drivers from the Palampur volunteer camp, met me off the train, and we set off in a big white 4x4. At the other side of the town we came to the checkpoint between the states of Punjab and Himachal Pradesh. Sunil stopped to show some papers, and we crossed the border. Immediately on the Himachal side was a shed labelled 'English wine and beer shop'. I was to see these little shops selling alcohol all over the state. Although alcohol could be bought in Rajasthan it was not sold so openly.

We drove between fields of cereal crops, some green with young plants, others gold and ready for harvest. Mango trees were heavy with white blossom. There were wooded hills and blue mountains on the horizon. Excitement overcame my sleepiness. I was about to travel up from the plains into the foothills of the great mountains that I had dreamed of ever since I was a child.

It was not raining anymore, but it was much cooler and damper here. We stopped for breakfast at half past eight. Sunil had brought me cheese sandwiches, a hard-boiled egg and a banana, and the little café where we stopped provided plenty of very welcome hot *chai*.

The road began to climb and zig-zag upwards. Fields were replaced by cultivated terraces, and shabby little villages with wooden houses clung to the hillsides. Jagged snow-covered peaks appeared in the distance. Then the road ran beside a stony riverbed, and we entered a steep-sided gorge. A pink temple stood on a rocky outcrop above the fast-flowing stream. There were monkeys sitting on rocks and walking along the road beside us.

"Monkeys go for temple," Sunil said. "They get food."

We climbed steadily higher through a mountain landscape and eventually emerged onto a high plateau. At a road junction a signpost pointed to Dharamsala to the left and Palampur to the right. I had heard of Dharamsala as the home of the Dalai Lama and the Tibetan government in exile.

The road was still climbing upward, with a great range of mountains now on our left – the Dhauladhar range, where the peaks reach heights of over 5,000 metres. The rocks were black and their summits iced with brilliantly white snow. We turned onto a single-track road. It was raining again, and there were tea plantations on either side, with women in saris picking leaves from waist-high bushes.

A few minutes later, shortly after midday, we arrived at a tall white building on a steep slope above a wide riverbed, and I was welcomed to the volunteer house with a red spot on my forehead and a cup of *chai*.

* * *

The volunteer 'camp' in Himachal Pradesh is a four-storey house on the edge of Bundla village, just outside the small town of Palampur, at an elevation of about 1,500 metres (just a little higher than the summit of Ben Nevis). The house stands on a rise overlooking the stony Neugal riverbed. Pine-clad hills rise around and behind it, and beyond them tower jagged snow-clad peaks, brilliantly white against a blue sky on fine days, looming half hidden behind grey clouds on others. To the south-west, range after range of hills, becoming bluer and fainter with distance, cascade down towards the hot plains.

Snowstorms of white butterflies flutter in the bushes around the camp and then away across the road and over the valley. Everywhere I hear the sound of rushing water as tiny streams gush down towards the river. In the open space beside the camp tall stands of bamboo have been planted by the villagers – they use its strong stems, held together with rope, as scaffolding. Bushes are bright with red and yellow flowers that look like giant versions of the verbena I grow in the garden at home, and underfoot are tiny wild flowers I cannot identify, in gentian blue, daffodil yellow and white. Villagers walk along a little path shaded by trees, which provides a shortcut from their houses to the road.

There are so many birds here – mynahs and crows in the trees, Himalayan bulbuls sitting singing on the electricity wires, with a jaunty cap of feathers curling over their foreheads, tiny yellow-green warblers hiding in the foliage, and swallows and martins overhead. Every day a pair of kites patrols high above the river valley, and occasionally an Egyptian vulture joins them, easily identified by its pale wings edged with dark brown and its yellow head. Sometimes a beautiful flycatcher, turquoise blue from head to toe like the Bluebird of Happiness, perches at the top of a bamboo stand opposite the house, darting off to snap up an insect before returning to its perch. On one memorable occasion a pair of grey Indian hornbills flew into the tall trees nearby.

First thing in the morning a herd of sheep and goats is driven down the road by a woman in an orange sari, accompanied by a shaggy mongrel dog. The sheep come first – their tails hang down – and goats follow – with tails sticking up. I am usually woken by a series of clangs as monkeys leap from the trees, bounce off the corrugated iron roof of the outhouse and cross my balcony, peering in inquisitively through the windows. The young ones have a great game shaking the washing line, and sometimes a mother sits outside my window to clean her rather unwilling child.

We were warned not to look the monkeys in the eye, and when I met the gaze of a couple on my balcony as I tried to photograph them (from inside my room) they started shrieking and hurling themselves against the glass of the window. Monkeys can be a nuisance – they are endlessly on the prowl for food and, if they smell biscuits or sweets, little monkey fingers appear in a gap left by the warping of a balcony door as they try to get in. When some of them managed to get into a room through an insecurely closed window they trashed the place, opening boxes to strew the contents everywhere, and defecating on the beds.

One day the camp dog Kalu (Hindi for 'Blackie') confronted the big male leader of the troupe outside the front door. The monkey sat out of reach on the wall looking down at the dog defiantly, baring its teeth and clearly saying rude words in monkey language, and Kalu stood below barking furiously. Neither would give way, but finally the male monkey saw a young member of his family that he thought needed reprimanding, and he went off to see about it.

* * *

Every weekday morning the minibus took the narrow road up the hill from the fork in the village, crossing the small stream that cascaded down towards the river, then climbing up and up, more and more steeply, snaking across the mountainside, with a rocky cliff face on one side and on the other a sheer drop to the valley below. Across the valley in the hazy distance, beyond layers of hills, lay the plains.

Outside a tiny isolated shop with its back against the mountainside the minibus would stop to let us out. Accompanied by our executive from the camp, we would cross the road and climb down a steep and gravelly concrete path. Trees grew on our right, and on our left was a grassy verge above a shallow valley, where I sometimes saw the brilliantly white wings and streaming tail of a paradise flycatcher. But the bird always disappeared into the bushes before I could take a photograph.

Then we were level with the school roof, and a few more steps brought us down to the veranda which ran along the front of the three classrooms. From the veranda five or six steep narrow steps led down to the playground. At the far side the ground was level with the slate roofs of buildings lower down the slope. It had been shored up to make a flat area for the children to play on – the only horizontal piece of ground of any size on this hillside.

When we arrived the youngest children would be sitting in a row on the veranda chanting the Devanagari alphabet, which was painted on the outer wall of their classroom. One small child, in red and white gingham trousers and tunic, held a large wooden pointer, and as she indicated each letter the others shouted out its name and a Hindi word starting with that letter, like children in school at home reciting 'A for apple, B for ball…'. But when the volunteers arrived the whole school climbed down the steps to the playground – I was always worried that one of the small ones might trip and fall onto the hard earth at the bottom. They formed a circle, with a few scuffles to capture a prized position next to a volunteer, and sang the Good Morning song. Then we would start 'Heads, Shoulders, Knees and Toes', 'Twinkle, Twinkle, Little Star', or 'Old MacDonald had a Farm'. But very soon one of the older girls would say firmly "Class!", and they would rush off eagerly to start the day's lessons.

There were far more girls than boys at this government primary school, particularly in the higher classes. The headmaster, Anuj, explained to me that people sent their sons to private schools, but they were unwilling to spend money on a daughter's education. However, the state government in Himachal Pradesh has one of the best records in India for fostering education. From being regarded as an educationally backward state at Independence, the literacy rate has risen spectacularly for both men and women. By 1991 three-quarters of the male population of the state and just over half the women could read and write in at least one language, and this rose to ninety per cent of men and over three-quarters of women in 2011. This is in spite of the difficulties of providing schools in the mountainous and sparsely populated rural areas – and according to the 2011 census ninety per cent of the population of this state is rural.

The school was clearly much better funded than the one I taught in near Shiv. There thirty-one children were taught by a single teacher in one room. Here Anuj and four women taught just under fifty children in three classrooms. But like the teacher at Shiv, Anuj was very gentle and kind.

"I love my job," he said. "It makes me feel like a child myself to work with the children."

Two volunteers took class V (the top class), and Laura and I took children from classes III and IV together. The twelve children in this group sat at proper desks facing the blackboard on the front wall, and at the back of the room wood was stacked for heating during the cold winters. Slightly tattered posters hanging on the wall showed a map of India, fruit and vegetables, and a human body (wearing underclothes) with its head, hands and legs, ears, eyes and hair labelled in Hindi and English.

Most of my class were eight- and nine-year-olds but two seven-year-old boys, Ajay and Ravi, were promoted from second class as they were clever and keen to learn. They were shy, and Ajay hid his face in his hands when I asked him a question, but he picked up new words quickly and was good at arithmetic. For the first week or so Sangita's small brother insisted on coming to class with her. He was from the babies' class and would sit down next to Ajay and Ravi. His teacher would come to fetch him back, but a little later he would escape from her and appear in my classroom again. Anuj said:

"He tries to go to your class because he wants to be taught by a volunteer."

Sita was a slim, tidy little girl – but of course none of the children there was overweight. She and most of the other girls had their long dark hair in bunches, tied with scarlet or white ribbons. They wore school uniform – on one day white blouses and navy gym tunics, and on another red and white gingham trousers and tunics. The boys wore navy trousers and white shirts, or fawn trousers with blue shirts. But the weather was not yet hot, and some of the children wore their own wool sweaters on top of their uniforms. There had been torrential rain the day before I arrived, and many children had not gone to school that day because they did not have waterproof coats. In Rajasthan the schools are on holiday when the weather is hot and return when the monsoon lowers the temperatures, but here the school holidays are during the monsoon.

The children were enthusiastic, and keen to answer questions or come up to write on the board. When I handed out worksheets I found it hard to keep up with them. Sita usually finished hers first and, while I was sitting next to her marking it, others would clamour for me to come and correct their work. They wanted so much to be given lots of ticks and have 'Good', or even better 'Very good', written at the bottom of their paper.

Kamla, an attractive girl who looked slightly older than the others, had learning difficulties. She seemed to find it impossible to remember anything for more than a couple of minutes, and wanted Laura or me to sit beside her and help her with her worksheet. She was desperately anxious to get her answers right.

"As a child she once had an illness and almost died. This has affected her development," Anuj explained. "Her parents are not interested in her education, which makes it worse."

Another girl, Madu, had a severe lack of self-confidence which held her back. So Laura taught Kamla and Madu separately in a corner of the veranda, and they benefited from the personal attention.

Atul had rather Tibetan features, in common with several of the children in the school. Anuj warned me that he was 'a bit naughty', but I soon realised that he was another very bright child, who finished his worksheets quickly and then looked round for something else to do. He could never sit still in his seat while he waited for me to come to him, but walked round to see what the other children were doing, though he was never disruptive.

Indian children are expected to sit quietly in their places in school and are labelled 'naughty' if they move around or chat. One morning, when several of the class were talking while I attended to another child, Alka, our executive, came in and stuck strips of sellotape over their mouths to keep them quiet. The children were not at all upset by this but thought it a great joke and made no attempt to take the sellotape off again.

When I gave them paper and crayons most of the children started by drawing a line of jagged triangles across the top – the mountains. Monika always drew a sun peeping out between two of the peaks, and several of them would draw a long blue snaky path down from the mountains which, they explained, was the river. The children in Rajasthan never drew mountains and rivers – they knew only the flat, dry, sandy desert. They loved to draw peacocks, which the children here in the mountains never did, but all the children, in Rajasthan and Himachal Pradesh, drew flowers.

To help us plan lessons Laura and I set the children a short test. It helped us discover the range of their English vocabulary, and showed that, though they had learnt to use carrying in addition sums, most of them had difficulty with it. The exception was Atul. He rapidly completed all his sums correctly, and so I gave him a few more difficult ones, involving three-figure numbers instead of just two-figure ones, to keep him quiet until the others had finished. When I returned to him he had realised that he could invent his own sums and was correctly adding, with carrying, numbers in the thousands, tens of thousands and hundreds of thousands. Anuj was very impressed when I showed him Atul's paper and said that his class teacher had not realised he was so good at Maths.

Later I showed Atul how to use borrowing in subtraction. At first he looked a little puzzled, though he dutifully went through the operations I showed him. Then suddenly he understood it and looked up at me with an excited smile spread over his face. Moments like this made teaching these children a deeply rewarding experience.

* * *

In the village where the road forked I waited with Grete, a Norwegian volunteer of about my own age, for one of the public taxis to take us into the town. They did not run to any timetable, but we did not have to wait long before a white jeep appeared, already packed with people from higher up the hill. We clambered in at the back, joining an elderly man, three teenage lads and a young boy in seats facing each other, intended for two people on each by the makers of the vehicle. When one of the lads pulled the boy onto his lap, a lady in a pink sari squeezed in as well. The two rows of seats facing forward were already so full that the man next to the driver was leaning on his shoulder and seriously hampering his ability to change gear. Each passenger was charged ten rupees when we all got off at the main square, where the statue of a local dignitary was draped, like a Christmas tree, with glittering golden garlands.

In the post office Grete wanted to post a parcel. She had been in Himachal Pradesh for some weeks and, now in April, the weather was beginning to get warm, so she was sending her winter clothes home. She already had the parcel sewn up in white cotton ready to post, but bureaucracy had increased since I had posted my parcel home from Shiv, or perhaps in Himachal Pradesh the regulations were stricter. Whatever the reason, Grete was given four long forms to fill out, and when she returned two unfilled because they were duplicates of the others she was told that two copies of both forms were essential. Eventually the process was completed, while those behind us in the queue peered curiously over our shoulders, and the parcel was handed over. I was glad to hear later that her parcel arrived safely in Norway, for none of the postcards I sent from that post office ever reached my family and friends.

Sometimes I walked down to the town. In the village, past the fork in the road, was a tiny open-fronted shop advertising itself as 'Krishna Ladies Tailor'. Krishna loved a chat. He invited me in to sit at the back, while his wife fixed the hem of my scarf, and proudly showed me an album of photographs of himself and his wife with past volunteers, and of his teenage son and daughter who both attended the local secondary school. The shop was stacked with swatches of brightly coloured material, and finished clothes on hangers adorned the back wall. Near the doorway, where the light was good, his wife sat at her treadle sewing machine, with pictures of fashionable *salwar kameez* pinned to the wall behind her.

When I left Krishna's shop I went on down, past the temple, with the picture on its gate showing a blue four-armed goddess waving a bloody severed head, and past the forge near the end of the village, where a man worked strips of metal into elaborate gates and railings.

Below the village the road ran through tea plantations. Tall trees grew in the midst of the tea bushes, some in flower with sky blue or golden yellow blossoms, and parakeets shrieked and squabbled in the branches. Concrete channels provided irrigation, and in some places the bushes were growing round huge boulders.

Women in saris picked the leaves and filled woven baskets which they balanced on top of the bushes.

One day I visited the co-operative tea factory and saw a tractor and trailer delivering fresh green leaves. Inside, on the first floor, the leaves were spread in huge rectangular wooden trays for twenty-four hours. Then men climbed into the trays and filled baskets with the leaves. Carrying a laden basket on his head, each man in turn stood on a large weighing machine, while a clerk at a desk in the corner recorded the weights. Then the leaves were tipped onto the floor and brushed through a hole to the drying room below. There the leaves were tossed by machines and heated to a hundred degrees centigrade. This relatively low temperature produces the delicately flavoured tea that they describe as green gold.

The tea is not used for making *chai* but is simply infused with hot water. Although the leaves appear black when they are dry, they become green when moistened. I developed a taste for this tea, which is neither black tea nor yet quite like any green tea I have ever tasted. I have looked for it since I returned home. A speciality tea shop in Dublin sells 'Grand Himalaya' tea, but it is not quite the same.

After the tea plantations the road turns, passing the church of Saint John in the Wilderness and emerging in the sudden bustle of the town square. From there the long main street leads downhill, thronged with pedestrians, mopeds, motorbikes and the occasional car, till it reaches the bus station at the bottom. Looking back up the hill, snow-clad peaks tower high above the dusty buses and the tiled roofs of the town.

At the top of the street, near the main square, is the Joy coffee bar (advertising itself as 'Pure vegetarian') where I drank refreshing mango *lassi* (a chilled flavoured yogurt) or iced coffee (which was a coffee milkshake). A little way further down, a road to the left leads to a small square where *tuk-tuks* and taxis wait for custom.

On the corner I bought juicy ripe mangos from a small fruit stall, before taking a *tuk-tuk* back to camp.

Down the main street were stores selling the local woollen shawls, woven in neutral colours and edged with geometric patterns in rusty shades. There were shops with arrays of spices in little bowls, shops selling sweets, biscuits and groceries, numerous pharmacies, and even a bookshop. I bought an attractive bag in navy cotton, decorated with elephants and flowers in appliqué studded with sequins, and another covered with blue and green floral embroidery in wool.

Many shops sold nothing but bangles and *bindis*, but it was difficult to find any bangles to fit over my knuckles – the hands of Indian women are small and delicate. Eventually, at the very back of his shop, a man pulled out a single set of larger bangles, which were not only wide enough to go over my hands but were coloured in gold and peacock, a perfect match for my sari.

I was always tempted by the displays of material for making *salwar kameez*. The packs were arranged to show the decorated neck part of the *kameez*, and provided material for the *salwar* (trousers) and scarf in contrasting colours. I could not resist a bottle green *kameez* embroidered with a spray of big orange and white flowers with golden stems and leaves, teamed with navy *salwar* and a navy and green scarf.

I took this material, and the turquoise material that Subhadra had given me, to the tailor's smart glass-fronted shop. The lady who presided recorded my measurements in a book. She decreed how long the sleeves should be, how tight the bust, and how the trousers should be fitted at the ankle, reaching almost to the ground, so that I was afraid of catching my foot in them and tripping. When I returned to collect my new outfits she directed me to a tiny cupboard at the back to try them on. Inside it was hot and airless, and I was sticky by the time I had struggled into the tight tunics. She was disapproving when I asked her to make them slightly less tight – a tight fit is fashionable – but called to one of the girls sitting at a machine and told her to adjust the seams.

In a small arcade I found a shop selling lengths of material for scarves. The cloth was white, and some had gold threads across at intervals. I provided a small scrap of material from my new turquoise *salwar kameez*. The scarf material I had chosen was sent away to be dyed and came back the next day a perfect match.

* * *

On the day of the wedding to which I had been invited I arrayed myself in all my finery – my beautiful peacock blue and gold sari, gold and peacock earrings, a three-inch-long row of gold and peacock bangles on each arm, and a peacock bindi on my forehead. (I had some help with the sari from girls at a local hotel where the bride's family and friends were staying.) Mani, the elderly lady who worked in the kitchen at the camp, gave me a thumbs up sign when she saw me. Grete and several other volunteers were going too. They had not got invitations but were encouraged to go by some of the Indian staff who had been invited. Indians are lavish with impromptu invitations to weddings, as I had noticed on my original tour when several of our group were invited to join a wedding celebration in the hotel where we were staying. So that afternoon a group of us stood on the steps outside the volunteer house waiting for the taxi to take us to the wedding on the opposite side of the town.

My invitation was for half past five, with the religious ceremony due to start at six. But when we reached the wedding venue shortly before six only a few other guests had arrived. The front of the building was decorated with pink, orange and yellow bunting, and we walked in along a corridor decorated in the same colours, then out across a veranda into a large open-air space with its walls covered in the same pink and orange bunting.

All round the sides were long tables, behind which chefs were preparing to serve food. One man was carefully arranging a display of beautiful fresh fruit – pineapples, pears, apples, grapes and mangos. Down in the far corner a bar was being set up. In the centre was a large open-sided pink and orange marquee, where chairs draped in white were set around tables covered with pink and orange cloths. Waiters plied us with soft drinks and spicy titbits.

I watched the priest preparing for the ceremony in a square area of the veranda marked out by four red and gold pillars. They supported a canopy from which hung long tassels of yellow flowers. He was lighting incense sticks at a low table decorated with marigolds and putting out small bowls full of what looked like grains, seeds and flowers. His saffron robe covered one shoulder, and under it he wore a green and white striped Aertex shirt.

At last the guests were called to welcome the bride and groom. We stood in the entrance corridor, Indians along one side and Europeans along the other. The wedding car appeared – a white jeep, studded all over with yellow and orange marigolds, and other flowers in pink and white. There was a great wreath of pink flowers on its bonnet and another on the roof. It drew to a halt at the doorway, and we had our first sight of the bride and groom, dressed in dazzling scarlet and gold. She looked like a princess from the *Arabian Nights*, in a gold sari decorated with embroidery and little flowers made of gold and silver beads. There were streaks of scarlet in the draperies over her shoulder and in her headdress, her arms were encased in gold and scarlet bracelets, and there were red stones in her gold jewellery – a necklet hanging almost to her waist, dangling earrings, and a medallion falling from her headdress onto her forehead. From one of her earrings a jewelled chain lay across her cheek and was linked to a golden hoop in her nose. The groom was almost as gorgeous – he wore a white satin tunic embroidered with gold and small bright beads, with a scarlet collar decorated with jewels. His headdress was scarlet, with a golden bejewelled panel at the front and several pale golden streamers falling on either side of his face.

Bride and groom stood at the door while first their fathers, and then their mothers, exchanged marigold garlands and marked each other's foreheads with red powder. Then they processed between the rows of guests, as we showered them with sweetly scented rose petals. They took off their shoes and entered the temple area, to sit cross-legged on cushions in front of the low table. At one side sat the priest, chanting in Sanskrit and performing mysterious rites with the contents of the bowls. A little fire was lit and after some time the bride and groom, linked together by a yellow ribbon, got up and walked around the pillared area and the fire. They made the circuit seven times in all, but by this time most of the Indian guests had drifted away to chat and eat and drink, and secular music was blaring from loudspeakers. Only the Europeans and the close family were left watching the ceremony.

Pankaj, whom I knew from Jaipur, came up to me and said:

"This will be going on for another hour or more, so come and have something to eat."

So I wandered with Grete past the array of food being cooked at the tables along the side, tasting a piece of spiced chicken on a cocktail stick here, and a vegetable rissole dipped in a piquant sauce there, and drinking Kingfisher beer from the bar. Young Indian men would come up and engage us in conversation, but Sunil and the other drivers from the camp, who were among the guests, were very protective and would come along every so often to check on who we were talking to, and once to intervene when a rather drunk man lurched towards us. I was touched by their care for us, though it was unnecessary – the young men were extremely polite, and interesting and pleasant to talk to.

Eventually the religious rites came to an end, and bride and groom mingled with their guests. I managed to congratulate them in Hindi. The priest shed his saffron robe and came to chat with us and pose for a photo, wearing Western trousers and his green and white striped shirt.

The bride and groom and their close families mounted the low platform of an orange and pink bower, where a gilded couch stood. Because the bride was European, the proceedings were adapted to include speeches by the two fathers. They both spoke in English, praising their children and the close ties that now united their families and their countries, and praying for good luck for the married couple, and success in their project to open an orphanage.

Then fireworks exploded into flowers and waterfalls of green and gold and white above us, as the bride and groom placed marigold garlands around each other's necks. Seated on the gilded couch they received the congratulations and gifts of their guests, who queued up to mount the steps to the platform and have their photographs taken with the newly married couple.

As people dispersed to talk, eat and drink, Sunil urged me to come and dance. In a large hall inside the building Indian music blared from a corner behind a small dancefloor, and yet more food was being prepared at tables along the walls. Sunil encouraged me onto the dancefloor packed with people. Nobody actually danced with the same partner – or even any partner – for long, and I found myself dancing in front of first one person, then another, and sometimes in a group with two or three others. It was a little like the jive or the twist of my youth, but Indians dance with their arms and hands as well as their feet, and I tried to imitate them. Apart from the volunteers, most of the dancers were young men and children, though there was one young Indian woman there who smiled at me and danced with me for a while.

As I retired from the floor to catch my breath one young man I had danced with several times asked me to come back again. When I claimed exhaustion he pleaded:

"I ask you as my mother."

How could I refuse?

An older man danced with me, and when I left the floor to rest for a moment he said:

"Come and meet my wife. She is sitting over there. Perhaps she will join the dancing if you ask her."

She was sitting in the rows of chairs in the centre of the room, and after a little polite conversation I asked her if she would come and dance. She joined me on the dancefloor, the only older Indian woman there, and was soon lost in the maze of dancers. But when I caught a glimpse of her through the crowd she was smiling and clearly enjoying herself.

At last I could manage it no more and retreated to choose some Indian food from the array of European and Indian dishes on offer. As I sat to eat, I was joined by the young woman I had met on the dancefloor.

"I used to work at the volunteer camp as an executive," she told me. "I found the work the volunteers were doing so inspiring that I decided to become a teacher. I am at teacher training college here now, and I shall be fully qualified in a year's time."

Later, back outside, there was a cake-cutting ceremony, and I met Anuj, the headmaster from my school, with his wife and seven-year-old daughter.

"The sari suits you. You look just like an Indian woman, apart from the skin colour," he said. But now the organised celebrations seemed to be over, and Grete and I decided it was time to go home. Sunil insisted on selecting a taxi driver that he felt was reliable, and we escaped, like Cinderellas, at midnight.

* * *

In one of my photographs children are climbing up a steep narrow path in the red earth between pine trees. The little girls are in their uniform of white blouses and faded navy gym tunics, while the boys have white shirts, navy trousers and striped school ties. Some of the children are so small that I want to pick them up and help them up the slope. The headmaster, solid and comfortable, encourages them onward and upward. The whole school is going on a picnic.

At the top of the hill we emerged onto a paved road. The children were grouped in threes, holding hands, and I had a string of three on either side, holding my hands. Whenever the children heard a motorbike coming they would cry, "Side!", and all stood on the grass beside the road until it had passed. A little further on we came to a pump, and one of the bigger boys heaved on the handle while the rest took it in turn to catch water in their two hands and drink.

As we walked the children chatted to me, pointing out their houses:

"Sangita's house."

"My house."

Then in Hindi, pointing to a small shack:

"*Vah dukan hai* (That is a shop)."

One little girl said:

"*Bahut dur hai* (It is a very long way)."

It was a two-kilometre walk, uphill all the way. Before we left, Anuj had picked out several of the smallest children who he thought would not be able to walk so far, and to their great disappointment they were left behind with one of the teachers.

The road twisted and turned up the hillside, with a steep drop to the valley below on our right. Then a pale stone tower appeared above the trees ahead, and there was a temple, perched on the edge of the precipice, with an open space in front of it. At one side of this space, under the pines, was a sandy area and a pump, where we took off our shoes and washed our feet. Then we went up the few steps into the temple, ringing the bell above the entrance to let the goddess (for this was a temple to Durga) know we were there.

Inside the gaudily decorated shrine, Durga looked out at us with glassy eyes and a fixed smile, dressed all in red and seated on a tiger. (Although I was always told that Durga's animal was a lion, this one had stripes and looked just like a tiger. When I asked what a tiger was called in Hindi the answer was always *sher*, which means lion, and I could never get anyone to tell me how lions and tigers are differentiated in Hindi. Kipling's tiger in *The Jungle Book* is called Shere Khan.) One of Durga's four hands was raised in blessing, and in another she held a trident.

The children crowded at the rail in front of the shrine to be blessed by the priest. Then he handed out a *dholak* (a small drum) and a *chimta* – this was an instrument made from two long metal strips hinged together at one end, with a row of little cymbals attached to each strip. The headmaster spread a big mat on the floor, and the children sat and sang hymns to Durga while he beat the drum, and Viren, the camp executive who was with us, played the *chimta*. After a short while half a dozen young men – probably in their early twenties – joined us and took over the musical instruments. They were expert with them, and the singing became more vigorous, the children started to clap in time to the music, and then we were all standing up and dancing, the children with great smiles on their faces.

Finally the music stopped, the young men returned the instruments to the priest, and we took the children outside for their picnic. They sat in two rows, cross-legged on the ground, while we handed out bananas, biscuits and little cartons of mango juice with straws to drink it through. Each child said politely, "Thank you, ma'am," as I handed out the snacks. (It was only a snack as they would be given their usual free school lunch when they got back.) The cartons of juice were a great novelty – they had never had a drink like that before.

With the picnic over, the headmaster gathered up the empty cartons and banana skins in a bag, and we retrieved our shoes and set off home. The children were tired and happy. One very small girl had not eaten her biscuit. She told me she was going to take it home for her baby brother. So I secretly gave her another one for herself as we said goodbye outside the school.

* * *

Pine trees cloaked the slopes on the opposite side of the river where I wandered one warm sunny Saturday afternoon. As I walked, hundreds of tiny brown frogs jumped from the grass beside the path into puddles left by an overnight thunderstorm to hide beneath the water with only their eyes above the surface watching me pass. I saw one of them leap up to catch a butterfly. The pines were being tapped for their resin, with conical cans attached to each trunk below a scar where the bark had been removed. Swallows soared and darted after insects, and the green parakeets had charcoal grey heads, unlike the green-headed rose-ringed ones which frequented the village and the tea plantations. On a tree trunk I saw the black and white barred backs of a pair of woodpeckers with golden yellow crowns and a scarlet patch on the nape of the male.

Once again I heard the strange call that had been puzzling me since I had arrived in the mountains – a strange monotonous 'peehoo peehoo peehoo' which went on and on for minutes at a time. Was it really a bird? One of the executives suggested I was hearing the sound of conches from the temple.

It was several weeks before I finally identified it as a bird, when one came to perch in a tree outside the volunteer house. It was a large untidy looking creature with a heavy bill and a confusion of brown, yellow and green plumage. It looked as though it had got dressed too rapidly in an assortment of coloured rags. This was a great barbet, and I was delighted to have seen it, since my bird book said that it hid in foliage, making it hard to get a glimpse of it.

On another occasion the dog Kalu decided to accompany us as I walked with Grete and another volunteer across the river and up the hillside beyond. From the bridge below our house we looked upstream to see, away near a bend in the river, the narrow jet of a waterfall leaping from the cliff top and plunging hundreds of feet to the river valley below.

We climbed up towards a village where houses perched on either side of a deep cleft, through which a stream ran down to join the river. Women carrying huge bundles, some of sticks and others of leafy branches, greeted us. Leaving the road we struck off along a rough path which led us steeply up, almost through the courtyard of a house, and rejoined the road after it had meandered back and forth with many a hairpin bend.

A man with a tiny store selling refreshing cold drinks chatted to us, and called to three more women carrying bundles of sticks to come to be photographed. Here we had reached a little plateau, where corn was growing in patches between the trees, and we looked across to cultivated terraces on the slope beyond.

The houses were thinly spread, but there must have been a sizeable population round about as we came across a big new two-storeyed secondary school. Slogans painted on its walls, in Hindi and English, read 'Intelligence without ambition is a bird without wings', and 'It is good to think well, it is divine to act well'.

The road seemed to be taking a long way round to cross the stream running through the cleft, so we branched off again, down the side of the valley, to where we could see a little stone bridge. A cow mounted the steep flagged path towards us, and three boys joined us, asking our names and wanting to be photographed, but left us when we crossed the bridge and climbed up to the houses of the village on the opposite side. A black water buffalo lounged outside one house, and a man sat beside the road cleaving huge rocks, which fell apart to show a white interior speckled with black and grey, like a very pale granite.

We followed the road downward, to where a metal bridge crossed the cleft close to where the stream flowed into the river. From there it was a short walk back to the bridge over the river and up the hill to our house. Kalu had followed us all the way, occasionally turning aside to investigate an interesting scent, and flopped down in front of the house to rest when we reached home again.

* * *

In the afternoons Rikki, my executive, and I set off for our English class in a one-roomed community hall on the edge of the town. There had been no volunteer available to take it for some weeks, and only two or three children turned up during my first week. So we spent one afternoon advertising our services around the neighbourhood.

As we walked steeply down towards the river Rikki saw two children of an appropriate age outside a house, and led me in, past a couple of men bending the ends of long iron rods in the courtyard, to a large empty room. We could see a group of women at the door of a room beyond, and one of them, who turned out to be the children's mother, came forward and greeted us. Rikki explained our mission in Hindi, and she offered us plastic chairs to sit on and called her husband, while the children – a boy and a girl – told us their names and that they were seven and eight years old. Their father appeared in a smart white *kurta* and trousers.

"I want my children to take English lessons. They were going, but the classes stopped. I did not know they were starting again," he explained.

Their mother brought us *chai* and tiny *pakoras*, and Rikki and the parents spoke together in Hindi. I could follow what they said well enough to remind Rikki that he had not told them it would be the following Monday that classes resumed. Then with polite thanks from us, and assurances from the parents that the children would attend our class, we left, past the men still working on the iron rods, and went on down the hill.

There were children playing in the courtyard of a small temple, and when Rikki spoke to a girl and her brother they left their game to lead us to their house and call their mother. It was a rather ramshackle building on a narrow, dirty alley, but the mother was very elegantly dressed in a smart *salwar kameez*, and when she understood our reason for calling she invited us in. The room we entered was small, with a baby asleep on a big double bed which occupied most of the space. A crowd of other children peered at us from an inner doorway. We refused her offer of *chai*, and left. Now we had two more recruits for our class.

Further on a group of women and children were sitting on a balcony above the river, and we stopped to talk to them. Several of the older children showed an interest in our class, so we decided that if all those we had spoken to came along we would have as many pupils as we could manage. Indeed the attendance rocketed the following week, but the range in ages, from seven to fourteen, made holding a class difficult. Luckily a new volunteer, Emmy, joined us, and we were able to split the group according to their language ability.

The children enjoyed word puzzles. One bright little eight-year-old boy, whose English was very good, managed to find additional words in a square array of letters by drawing a jagged path through them, or altering a letter here and there to fit his needs. They all loved drawing, and after they had finished the puzzles and exercises in English we would hand out paper and crayons, and they would spend the rest of the time leaning over their papers on the floor, concentrating on their art work.

One afternoon, while they were all busy drawing, a very small girl with her hair tied up in plaits appeared at the door.

"*Apka nam kya hain* (What is your name)?" I asked her, expecting her to be very quiet and shy.

But she answered loudly and confidently, and came to sit between a boy and girl.

"She is our cousin," the boy told me.

When I asked her age in Hindi she said:

"*Dus* (ten)."

"No, she is really only three," said her cousin.

I gave her paper and crayons, and she sat between her cousins, drawing happily.

The afternoon always finished with songs and games, and they loved the Hokey-Pokey. Then they would sing the Goodbye Song, and Rikki, Emmy and I would go back to the road to be picked up by the camp minibus.

* * *

Two hours away by bus, along a road running parallel to the snow-clad peaks of the Dhauladhar mountains, was Dharamsala (which they pronounce Dharamshala). This large town, on the floor of a wide valley, is associated in Western minds with the Dalai Lama. But that is not where he lives. His residence, and the home of the Tibetan government in exile, is in the village of Mcleodganj, which clings to the steep hillside over a thousand feet above the town. One Saturday I set off to spend a weekend there, accompanied by Annika and Wenke, two 'grown-up' Scandinavian volunteers.

In the village streets of Mcleodganj, Buddhist monks and nuns in deep rust-red robes mingled with other Tibetans and Western tourists. Most of the few Indians around were shopkeepers or hotel employees. We had no chance of seeing the Dalai Lama himself as he was away on a tour of the United States and Europe.

As we entered the precincts of the Tibetan museum and monasteries, a large board reminded us of the eleventh Panchen Lama, whose twenty-third birthday had been celebrated the week before. The board named him 'The world's youngest political prisoner' and explained in English and Hindi that he had been taken away to China soon after he was recognised as the reincarnation of the Lama, in 1995 at the age of six, and had not been seen since.

From the quiet and peaceful grounds of the monastery, shaded by trees, Wenke, Annika and I looked down on the town of Dharamsala far below. Beyond it, the plain stretched into the hazy blue distance, but to our right, on the steep slope, we glimpsed white houses with red roofs peeping out between trees. Beyond were forested hillsides with snow-clad peaks towering above them.

The yellow monastery buildings are on several levels, and we climbed up steps, spinning the gilded prayer wheels on our right as we approached the doors of a temple. Entering, I was confronted by a terrifying gilded statue with many arms and a demonic expression. This tantric deity, Kalachakra, seemed to me an anachronism in that peaceful place. But Tibetan Buddhism has transformed ancient gods into essences or archetypes, to be meditated upon and aspired to rather than appealed to for divine help. Kalachakra personifies cycles of time and represents the omniscience of the Buddha. Nearby was his consort Visvamata, also many-armed and horrifying in appearance. In contrast to these violent images, Buddhist monks in a far corner were silently and devotedly creating a mandala, scraping coloured stone onto tiny areas of the intricate design.

The great golden image of the Buddha above the altar looked down on bowls of purifying water and a row of butter lamps. Offerings had been left on all available surfaces – Cadbury's chocolate bars, packets of biscuits and sweets, and little cartons of fruit juice. Outside, in a small room with windows on all sides, a monk was busy lighting hundreds of butter lamps.

That evening we attended a bizarre Tibetan music and dance event in a drab school hall, where we sat on wooden boards raised a few inches off the floor on bricks. The audience was very small – apart from ourselves there was only a young Western couple, but a Tibetan woman with three or four children sat at the back.

The young Tibetan man, who turned out to be the sole performer, started by telling us about his escape from Tibet twelve years before:

"When I was a teenager my family and others from our village decided we must leave Tibet. We took only what we could carry, and set off, avoiding roads and keeping to mountain tracks. We only walked at night, and we dared not use a light because we were afraid of being stopped by the Chinese. In the dark we often tripped and fell, and were covered with scrapes and bruises.

"Finally we reached the bridge between Tibet and Nepal and crossed it. We celebrated and were very happy, even though the Nepalese put us in prison. But India agreed to accept us as refugees, and so we were able to negotiate our release.

"India has been very good to us. It has provided me and other young Tibetans with a good education in Indian schools. This has given us the chance to live and work in India and elsewhere. Some have got jobs in the US, and others in Europe. My younger brother is studying in Delhi, but I decided to stay here to look after my mother. I studied Tibetan culture, and now I give performances of Tibetan song and dance."

Then he started to sing, and the Tibetan woman and children at the back of the room joined in. Dressed in a black knee-length robe with gold trimmings, and blue sneakers, he danced to music from a CD player on the floor behind him. The music was unfamiliar and, to my ears, monotonous. His dancing, in the flickering light of the candles he had lit, was hypnotic. He finished the first half of his programme by spinning round and round very fast for five minutes or more, but he showed no signs of dizziness.

After the interval the performance departed from strictly traditional Tibetan dance, and he invited audience participation. Each of us in turn was whirled about till we were breathless. When it came to the turn of the young couple, he took one over each of his shoulders and spun them round and round. His solo finale was an angry devil dance, very strenuous and acrobatic. It ended with a fire dance, in which he lit strips of paper from the candles on the floor behind him and weaved flaming patterns in the air. At the end he thanked us all for coming and hugged each one of us.

The next morning we decided on some gentle exercise and set out up the hill. Little stalls offered jewellery and wooden blocks for fabric printing. Near the top of the village several bigger hotels catered for trekkers, who set out from here to climb up to the snow line and beyond. At this height stately deodars (Himalayan cedars) were beginning to replace the pines. A small temple dedicated to Shiva was the worshipping place for a Ghurka regiment stationed there in the nineteenth century. A man was praying, standing in the water at the edge of the small tank in front of the temple. But beyond the tank, and separated from it only by a metal fence, was what looked like a European swimming pool, with young men in bathing trunks at the water's edge.

Beyond the village we wandered along a path cut into the hillside. To our left the ground rose steeply, with grass, and low bushes a little like heather, growing between the rocks. I found dainty white saxifrage in clefts of rock, and a white viola, yellow oxalis, and many other beautiful wild flowers whose names I did not know.

Ahead of us the valley narrowed, and our path led upwards towards the foot of a waterfall that plunged vertically down to the mountain stream which flowed below us on our right. I watched women far below me doing their laundry in the stream, some scrubbing a carpet which was spread out on the rocks. Children splashed and played in a deep pool nearby. The Buddhist care for the environment was marked by a stone slab, on which was painted the exhortation 'Together let's clean the planet'. (In another Buddhist monastery and village nearer camp, I had seen a No Smoking sign, with the caption 'Enjoy smoke-free environment' and announcing that the village was 'the first to be declared smoke free by the state government'.)

Prayer flags fluttered, white, blue, green, yellow and red, strung across the stream at the top of the waterfall. Close to the pool at its base tiny shacks sold soft drinks.

A group of cheerful chatty young men greeted us.

"Good morning, how are you? Where are you from?"

They were interested in what we were doing in India and what we thought of the country.

"We are from the Punjab," they told us. "It is hot there now, so we escape here to the mountains at the weekend whenever we can."

That afternoon we visited the museum. Outside it a great stone was set up, with the white peaks of mountains added round its edge in plaster. The whole centre had become a great sea in which plaster figures were drowning, their hands raised with clenched fists. Inside, exhibits told the sad and violent story of Tibet and its annexation by China. Upstairs were testimonies from various Tibetan leaders, all hopeful for the future against all the odds. I found that of the Dalai Lama particularly moving. He spoke of the Chinese without bitterness, and looked forward to a peaceful resolution of the conflict.

By the time I left the museum I was hobbling and finding it difficult to walk. While putting away my camera after lunch I had failed to look where I was going and had missed a step, coming down heavily on my right ankle. It was now very swollen and painful. Luckily for me the taxi driver, who was to take us down to the bus station at Dharamsala, offered to drive us all the way back to camp for little more than we would have paid on the bus. He spoke good English and chatted all the way back.

"I used to be a mountain guide," he said. "Many tourists take treks up the mountains from Mcleodganj. But now I have a wife and two children, so I felt it was better to be my own boss rather than working for someone else. As a taxi driver I can arrange my own working time and see more of my family."

He delivered us right to the door of the volunteer house.

* * *

On Monday morning I realised that I would not be able to walk down the steep path to school, even with the aid of my hiking stick. Alka, who was in charge at camp, packed me off to a hospital in the town, with Sunil to look after me.

"I'm sending you to a private hospital," she said. "There would be too many people waiting at the public hospital. You will be seen more quickly at this one."

The minibus dropped us off, and we walked up a path over a patch of grassy ground, to where two dismal grey concrete buildings faced one another across a covered area. There were padded benches in the space between the two buildings but no patients sitting there. If, as Alka had said, the public hospital was always overcrowded, this place was the opposite – it seemed completely deserted.

The electricity had failed, and the doctor beckoned to me with a torch. I entered his small, windowless office in one of the concrete blocks and sat in front of him. It was very dark, and the door remained open to let in what little light it could. His examination of my foot was helped when the lights suddenly came on again.

"I don't think anything is broken," was his verdict, "but you should have an X-ray to make sure."

He handed the X-ray request to Sunil, and we crossed to an open door in the building opposite, which had 'X RAY' in large letters on the wall above it. Inside, the dark room was fitted out with an X-ray machine above a couch, and a small curtained area for the radiographer. An old man was standing against the far wall to have his chest X-rayed. He was just skin and bone and looked very sick. When he had been X-rayed a young man waiting with him in the room picked him up in his arms and carried him across to the door into the main hospital building, next to the doctor's office.

Sunil stayed in the room with me while the radiographer took two X-rays of my ankle from inside his curtained area. He went away to develop the plates, and in a few minutes he came back with the still wet X-rays, which he gave to Sunil, who waved them around to dry them. I sat in the waiting area, where there was now one other patient, and Sunil took the X-rays to the doctor. Soon the doctor came out and told me I had damaged a ligament and would need the foot strapped up, and that I should rest it for seven days. Then I saw him drive off in a rather smart car.

After a short while I was taken into the treatment room and dispensary, and a young man put a gel on my foot and bound it up with a crepe bandage. My confidence in the treatment increased when I recognised the ingredients of the gel and tablets I was given as diclofenac, exactly what I would have expected to be prescribed at home. I was also given pills containing vitamins E and C – they seem keen to hand out vitamin pills here, and other volunteers with a variety of problems had also been given them.

My treatment was unbelievably cheap – 150 rupees for the X-ray (less than three euro) and 400 rupees for the consultation, bandaging and tablets. With my foot heavily bandaged I could not get my sandal on again, and Sunil lent me one of his to walk the short distance across to the road, where the minibus picked us up again.

During my week's enforced rest at the camp I tried to crystallise my thoughts about this area and compare it to the places where I had worked in Rajasthan. I had a long chat with Alka, who was a very independent young woman in her mid twenties. She told me that girls in Himachal Pradesh did not get married before they were twenty, unlike the fifteen-year-old brides in Rajasthan. She had visited the Lalsot camp and thought Rajasthan was very backward. It was she who told me that she had been extremely offended when, on a house visit, the host had asked her caste before deciding whether or not to offer her a seat. Clearly she felt that her position as a member of staff in the volunteer organisation should have been more important than her caste.

But caste was not irrelevant in Himachal either. Annika told me of a child at the daycare centre where she worked, who was always accompanied by her older, school age, brother. They were both dirty and poorly dressed, and their parents scavenged in the rubbish tips for a living. They were some of the lowest of the low in the caste system. We suspected that the boy did not go to school because he would have been discriminated against.

On the whole Himachal appeared much more prosperous than rural Rajasthan. The women were better dressed here, and the clothes I had bought for Lalsot and Shiv looked a little dowdy and plain, so I indulged in a couple of better outfits. On the way into town I passed several very smart houses, some with garages and cars. Farm houses were often large and freshly painted, and the one on the hillside opposite, that I could see from my balcony, had several buildings and was well maintained. I could watch a woman in a sari guiding several brown cows out to the steep pasture, or hanging washing in the yard.

A further sign of prosperity was a park down beside the river, with slides, roundabouts and swings, created by the local government. I had only seen a play area like this in the city of Jaipur, and that had been vandalised. This one was surrounded by a wire fence with gates which could be locked when there was nobody in charge. The children from Annika's daycare centre were brought to it one day. Several of them burst into tears when they were lifted into the camp minibus – this was a frightening new mode of transport. But they loved the park, and after an exciting and strenuous morning they fell asleep in the minibus on the way back to the centre.

Of course, in Himachal the climate is much better for agriculture than in Rajasthan. There is so much water coming down from the mountains. While I was there there were frequent thunderstorms at night, and rain showers on many days, though it was not the monsoon season. But the rain would clear quickly and the sun would come out. Although it grew pleasantly warm it was never really hot and dry as it had been in Jaipur a few weeks earlier, and I always needed the duvet at night. During my last couple of weeks, there was a heat haze over the land towards the plains so that I could not see the ranges of hills in that direction. Up here, where the British used to escape the heat of the summer on the plains, there was usually a pleasant breeze.

By now the fields of wheat, which had been dark green when I arrived, were golden and ready to harvest, and I was told that later in the year rice would be harvested. The terraces of wheat on the mountainsides made curving abstract designs, with golden swathes outlined in brown and green. As the harvest progressed sheaves of corn were to be seen, spread to dry on the terraces, beside the road, against fences and even on the roofs of buildings. One day there was a machine beside the road near my school, and people were feeding sheaves into it. It chopped the stalks up into small pieces and blew them out at the side. Women gathered the pieces into sacks for animal fodder in the winter. After the sacks had been filled, the verges of the road where the machine had been working were powdered with gold.

* * *

While I was resting my ankle I spent a lot of time preparing lessons. The bingo set that I made proved a great success, and even Kamla was able to recognise some of the numbers I called out. I had found two little picture books and translated one of them, *The Very Hungry Caterpillar*, into Hindi so that I could explain the story. Rikki, who was now my executive at school in the morning as well as at the afternoon class, had corrected my translation for me. None of the Indian staff knew a word for caterpillar in Hindi apart from *choti titeli*, meaning young butterfly, but they told me that in the local language it was *jhan*, so I used that.

Once more I realised that the children were not familiar with books for entertainment as opposed to school texts. They wanted to examine every page.

"Leaf", "strawberry", "cake", they cried, pointing to the pictures.

When we had gone through it once they wanted to read it all again, and then a third time, and they read it three times again the next day.

Over the weeks the children's English improved by leaps and bounds. Each of them could tell me something that they liked, usually something to eat, such as bananas, mangos or ice cream. Then Atul came up to the front of the class and announced, "I like singing," and soon they were jumping up from their places to show me that they liked dancing and running, hopping and skipping. I made them copy the new words from the board into their exercise books, and I introduced 'Here We Go Round the Mulberry Bush' during morning games, which brought in many more words with actions – brushing teeth, washing faces, getting dressed, eating breakfast and going to school.

At break Anuj handed out skipping ropes, and the children loved to count how many times they could skip before getting caught up in the rope. They played a variety of tag games, and both boys and girls played at houses. There was a tree standing at the school gateway which they used as a house, pretending to cook food and sweep the floor. One day the tree trunk was covered with ladybirds. Some of the boys scooped them up in handfuls and brought them to me. As soon as they were poured onto my lap they opened their wings and flew away.

The English girl who replaced Laura grew tired of skipping and playing energetic tag games with the children at break time. So she told them all to sit in a big circle with their eyes closed, and she would go round and try to make them blink or move. If they did they would be out. But it was a failure – no child moved a muscle. They all sat still in the pose for meditation, and nobody was called 'out'.

After my week's absence Sita asked anxiously:

"You last day?"

I reassured her that I would be there for three more weeks. But the following weekend I heard that my husband had to go into hospital for a serious operation, and so I cut short my time in India by two weeks and spent Saturday evening and Sunday trying to book flights home. On the Monday I had to tell Anuj and the children that it was my last day, as I would be leaving on Tuesday morning. Anuj was very kind and told me that I had brought the children on a lot while I was there, and he was sorry to lose me.

During the morning Anuj came into my class to explain to the children why I was going, and he asked them to say prayers for Brian. So they all put their hands together, closed their eyes and repeated some Hindi prayers after Anuj, and then a prayer in English so that I could understand. Then they had several minutes of silent prayer. Anuj said to me:

"I asked the children to pray for your husband because God listens to the prayers of children."

At break Atul made me sit by him outside, saying:

"You last day – no."

Then a whole crowd of my little girls, and one from the babies' class, came and sat round me and hugged me instead of going to play. When it was time for us to go to the minibus all my class and Anuj climbed up the path to the road with me, and the children picked the red flowers that grew wild everywhere and presented them to me. I found it hard to restrain my tears.

So on Tuesday morning I said farewell to the other volunteers and all the staff, patted Kalu, and was driven to the airport near Dharamsala. I watched tiny purple sunbirds feasting on the nectar of orange flowers in the bushes outside the terminal building. When the plane took off it seemed that the land fell suddenly and steeply away, so that the plane climbed only gently. Soon we were flying over the hot hazy plains towards Delhi, and I thought about the people I had met, and above all my lovely, bright, affectionate children. Saying goodbye to them was the hardest part of leaving, and I wondered whether I would ever get the chance to return.

Chapter 9

VOLUNTEERING IN KOLKATA

Back in India again for the first time in over two years, I luxuriated in the heat of Delhi and the spicy smell in the air. I watched black kites in the sky, mynahs strutting about on the ground, and a pair of long-legged red-wattled lapwings standing on a grassy patch by the road, as the bus took me from one terminal to the other.

I was reminded once again of the friendliness of Indian people. Even security officials at the airport will smile and chat. At the domestic terminal for my flight to Kolkata, the woman frisking me (everyone is frisked after passing through the arch of the metal detector) asked in Hindi how I was, and when I replied:

"*Main bahut achi hun*,"

she beamed and said:

"Very good. And what will you do in Kolkata?"

"I will be working with street children," I replied.

"That is a very good thing to do," she said as she waved me through.

* * *

After the villages where I had lived and worked, Kolkata struck me as very cosmopolitan – more so than what I had seen of Delhi, and much more so than Jaipur or the other towns I had visited in Rajasthan. Kolkata has many Italian, Chinese and other non-Indian restaurants. I lunched one day in the famous Flury's café in the city centre, where the door (opened by an attendant in European clothes) and some of the internal décor recalled its art-deco past. Flury's offered a full English breakfast, while the French café next door served croissants and patisserie.

Nearby I discovered a good range of children's books in English, in the Oxford Book Company. The shop would not have been out of place in the city after which it is named. I found smart shopping malls, with branches of European stores such as Marks and Spencer or United Colors of Benetton. And the monumental buildings in the city centre are all British, dating from the times of the East India Company and the Raj.

But this fourth trip to India as a volunteer was to be a new and heart-wrenching experience. In Palampur I had come across two children whose parents scraped a living scavenging on the town refuse heap, but in Kolkata hundreds of women and children toil on the city's enormous rubbish dumps. The children I had worked with in the villages were well cared for by parents or grandparents. But now I was to meet children who had been abandoned on the street, and others who had left their homes for a precarious and dangerous existence living by the railway.

Although the families I had met in the villages of Rajasthan and Himachal Pradesh were very poor, they lived in their own small houses. In Kolkata, with a population equal to that of the Republic of Ireland crammed into a city less than twice the area of Dublin[7], tens of thousands of people are homeless and maybe as

---

7 The population of the city, excluding suburbs, is close to 4.5 million in an area of 185 km^2, compared to Dublin city, excluding suburbs, with 527,000 in an area of 115 km^2.

many as two million live in slums. It is difficult to provide accurate figures as these people have no identity papers, and their births and deaths are not recorded.

On the streets of Dublin there are homeless people, mostly individuals, sleeping in doorways and begging during the day. In India homelessness is completely different. There are whole families living on the street. They do not just sleep there – they cook their food, eat, wash themselves and their clothes, and work on the street. At one crossroads I could cut off a corner by walking behind two fruit stalls, but people lived in this dusty space. Their washing was spread out to dry, and cooking pots were stacked away at the side. It was like walking through somebody's house.

As I walked home in the evening beside a busy main road I passed women squatting beside little stoves on the pavement, cooking their family's evening meal. Ragged children played around them, and a baby lay sleeping on a thin blanket. One family had two black goats tethered to the railings bordering the road, while a cockerel, a hen and two chicks roamed freely beneath the feet of hurrying pedestrians. These people were lucky – they made a living from small stalls on the pavement, where they sold fruit and vegetables or street food.

In spite of the numbers living on the street I saw very few beggars in the area where I lived and worked. But two elderly women sat on the pavement begging every day as I walked to the metro station. One wore the white sari of widowhood. Life on the streets for the old and sick is unimaginably hard. Mother Teresa recognised their need, and her foundation is still very active. I visited the Mother House, her convent, one afternoon – a place of deep peace, where I sat beside Mother Teresa's tomb, which was strewn with marigold flowers, and watched the nuns in their white and blue habits walking quietly from place to place. At the busy Kalighat crossroads I could always orient myself by looking for the enormous painting of Mother Teresa mounted on a building on the south-west corner.

The Hope Foundation[8], with which I volunteered, works with street and slum children. They run homes for boys and girls, a hospital, coaching centres where street children can drop in after school to do their homework and get academic help, and training centres for older teenagers and young adults. The Hope laundry, where I took my *salwar kameez* to be washed and ironed, was staffed by young men who had been taken by Hope from the streets and who would otherwise have had no useful trade. At the Hope café, where I ate lunch most days, young men and women were trained as chefs and waitresses, and on the floor above they could learn tailoring and other crafts.

I had seen the despair of an old couple in Rajasthan whose sons had all gone away to the city but had not succeeded in making enough money to help their parents left at home. So many of the people who leave the countryside, for what they think will be a better life in the city, do not have the skills necessary for employment in an urban environment. They end up merely scraping a living on the streets. Training schemes such as Hope's are very important for helping people out of the poverty trap. The only way children can hope for a better life than that of their parents is through education and training.

* * *

The apartment, which I shared with three other volunteers and an Indian member of Hope's staff, was in a warren of lanes off a big thoroughfare in the south of the city. Cars, buses, motorbikes and *tuk-tuks* streamed by on this main road, while the pavement was thronged with little stalls, roofed over with heavy plastic sheeting to protect them from the monsoon rains. Here was a man sitting cross-legged on the ground mending shoes, and just beyond him another was renovating an old pushchair. Behind them, sweet,

8 *The Hope Foundation Ireland*, http://www.hopefoundation.ie.

sickly-looking cakes were displayed in the glass window of a shop. Further on I stepped down into a tiny windowless room, where a cauldron of milk was perpetually simmering on the stove to produce the delicious yogurt that I bought there. At lunchtime people stood or sat on the ground between the street food stalls and the shops, eating platefuls of rice and curry. The pavements were often so cluttered that pedestrians braved the traffic and walked on the side of the road.

Many of the people who lived in this area were Muslim, and there was a small mosque beside the main road. The man who owned the yogurt shop was Muslim, and it could only be a Muslim who sold beef rolls, alongside vegetarian ones, at the big crossroads nearby.

As I turned off the main road, the traffic was left behind. I would meet thin brown hungry dogs, the occasional pedestrian, or a couple of boys on a bike. The street was edged with a dusting of white powder, laid to keep cockroaches out of the houses. On one lane I passed a covered stand where a man ironed clothes for a living, and after twisting and turning through the maze of streets I came to our local shop – four steps up to a counter displaying chocolates, biscuits, jam and other tempting treats. In the tiny room behind, the shelves round the walls were stacked with boxes and cartons of everything from drinking chocolate and tea to toothpaste and soap.

Two cheerful men behind the counter served me, and I bought milk, fruit juice, bread and water. (There was no purifier in the kitchen of the apartment, so we all drank bottled water.) As I got more adventurous and started cooking Indian meals in the evening I found that they had rice, lentils, garlic and onions in big sacks on the floor, and spices of all kinds in jars on the lower shelves. The shopkeeper was always amused when I asked for a single head of garlic, or what he considered a very small quantity of rice or dal. He would select a bag of a suitable size, neatly made from old newspaper, and pour in the rice or cumin seed that I asked for. Even the small white-shelled eggs were carefully placed in a newspaper bag, and I carried them home in my hand, afraid that they would break if I put them in my shopping bag.

* * *

It was holiday time for the festival of *Durgapuja* when I arrived in Kolkata, and even the metro was shut for the first week I was there. So my first few days were spent discovering the city and visiting some of the Hope boys' and girls' homes.

I had seen Durga revered as Goddess of the Harvest in Khajuraho, where bowls planted with rice seedlings were arrayed in front of the dark carved effigy of Durga in a tiny temple. In Himachal Pradesh we had taken the schoolchildren on an outing to a temple of Durga, where her brightly painted image was seated on a tiger. Here in Kolkata she is the Mother Goddess, and during her festival local communities build *pandals* to house her, and compete for prizes for the best decorated of these shrines.

As I was driven from the airport on the hot, dark, damp night that I arrived, colourful crowds thronged the city centre '*pandal* hopping' – going from one *pandal* to another to admire the decorations. The streets were spangled with coloured lights, and police stopped the never-ending stream of buses, taxis, cars and mopeds to allow crowds of pedestrians to cross the road, all dressed in their best, with excited children in family groups.

I went *pandal* hopping with other volunteers one afternoon. The biggest and most lavishly decorated were in streets not far from the city centre. I was surprised to see Disney-style images of Mickey Mouse and his friends on the inside as well as the outside of one. Another was decorated inside and out with a variety of musical instruments. Yet another took puppets as its theme, with fierce-looking gods and heroes displayed in miniature theatres round the outside. One was made to look like a fairy-tale palace, and another a three-tiered temple, painted blue with gold ornamentation and red tiled roofs. But inside each one was a statue of Durga, many-armed and fantastically attired, sometimes alone, at others accompanied by her sons, or, in one *pandal*, nine replicas of herself.

From the balcony of our apartment I could see the back of the small and relatively simple *pandal* set up by our local community. It completely blocked the lane and, although it was possible to squeeze past on foot in the space between it and the walls of the houses, it prevented cars or motorcycles from getting through. Inside the shrine, the figure of Durga, dressed and crowned in glittering green, blue and silver, stood on a demon, while her lion prowled at her feet. (It really was a lion here, with no tiger-like stripes.) In her eight hands she held a thunderbolt, a conch and several fearsome weapons. The demon was conquered by Durga when he grew too powerful in the land, and in Calcutta, the city created by the East India Company, and the capital of British India for many years, he represents British colonialism.

Every so often we would hear energetic drumming from the *pandal*. Early one morning the sound of drumming came closer, and looking out from the balcony I saw, approaching down the lane, half a dozen boys all beating drums, led by a man. He saw me watching, and when they were below my balcony he stopped the troupe and they performed a little dance to a complex and lively rhythm on their drums. I placed my palms together and bowed to thank them, and they proceeded on their way round the block.

The local organisers had collected money from all the neighbours to lay on a community lunch for three days of the festival. Our neighbour, a friendly grey-haired man, had invited everyone from our apartment, but we missed the first day. As we returned home that afternoon, we met him, and he greeted us with:

"Where were you? Why did you not come to lunch? You must come tomorrow."

So at one o'clock the next day Johanna, Samantha and I walked up the lane to where a long marquee had been set up behind the *pandal*. Just outside, tureens were bubbling on stoves, and young men stirred them and ladled out food into serving dishes. As one group of diners left others would take their places, and we were seated on a bench at a long wooden trestle. The table was cleared and wiped and re-covered with a clean paper cloth from a long roll. Then we were brought plates, plastic cups and paper napkins. But when another man came round to pour out water from a jug the neighbour who had invited us said:

"No, they must only drink bottled water."

He had warned us to bring our own water. The Indians tipped a little water into their hands and washed them before eating. Our plates were piled with yellow *khichari* (a mixture of rice and yellow lentils, on which the English kedgeree is based). Then we were served little cubes of spiced and fried potato, a mixed vegetable curry, and a little later a different potato curry.

It was very good food, but I was not very efficient at eating with my fingers, especially when the second course, of rather runny mango chutney and rice pudding with raisins and nuts, was brought round. One of the organisers said:

"They need spoons," and to our neighbour, "Why didn't you bring spoons for them? You must bring some tomorrow."

But we managed not to waste too much, and left with many thanks for the meal. Our hosts told us to come again the next day, and three ladies in magnificent saris who were just arriving stopped to greet us in good English and asked how we liked the food.

Next day we missed the lunch again, as we had been visiting the Hope hospital and arrived back too late. When we went to explain our absence and apologise, we were offered chairs in front of the *pandal* and served *chai* and biscuits. A microphone had been set up, and one after another people went up and sang – presumably hymns to Durga. Several of the local men chatted to us, and I discovered that our neighbourhood was a well-to-do area, where businessmen and their families lived, and many people spoke very good English.

After a while we realised that we were sitting with the men, and the women were in a different group, so we made our apologies and went home. But before we left we were invited to join the procession the next evening, when Durga was to be immersed in a local lake at the culmination of the festivities.

So the following afternoon we went down to the *pandal* to find out when the procession would start. There were no men in evidence this time, and we were welcomed by women, who smeared our cheeks and ears with red powder and placed a red stripe on our foreheads. Many of them were wearing red, because red is the colour of marriage and tonight Durga would be reunited with her husband, Shiva. (She is an avatar of Shiva's consort Parvati.)

Our neighbour's teenage granddaughter and some of her friends were practising dances for the evening's procession, to the drumming of the boys, and they insisted that we should join them. After a while I left the younger volunteers, Johanna and Samantha, to the dancing, and watched as women prepared Durga for her immersion. They placed leaves in her hands and wiped her face and the faces of her two sons, Ganesh and Kartikeya, who stood on either side of her. The light faded, and we went home for an hour or so, promising to return in time for the procession. As we left we were served *tiffin* – a snack of *puris* and potato, and a little white sweet.

In Kolkata the sun sets soon after five o'clock in October, so when we returned shortly after seven it was fully dark. Two large open-backed lorries were drawn up, one in front and the other behind the *pandal*, and there was much activity inside, with clouds of incense and insistent drumming. The man in charge of the event asked anxiously:

"Have you had your *tiffin*? We will not be back till very late."

As soon as we arrived we saw that the women had changed their saris and cleaned the red powder off their faces. Women with little heaps of red powder on metal plates were going round anointing everyone afresh. So we had to run home quickly to wash away the afternoon's streaks of red before having them re-applied.

Eventually the figures of Durga's two sons were brought out to the lorry in front of the *pandal*. Durga was taken out at the back and manhandled into the lorry waiting there, to the sound of furious drumming and the ululation of the women. One young man started to dance, contorting his body and rotating his arms through a full 360 degrees.

When the lorry carrying Durga drove round to the front of the *pandal* the girls we had been dancing with earlier called us to join them, and the procession started. At the front were the drummers, and then the crowd of local people, some dancing and others walking, followed by Durga's lorry with headlights full on and a bright lamp beaming down from the top of its cab. The second lorry, carrying Ganesh and Kartikeya, drove behind. Many people were dancing now – the young man who had started it, other men and women of all ages, and little children. The teenage girls urged us to join in, and the sweat streamed down my face in the hot, humid night. So I dropped back and walked with an older woman, who smiled and gestured to me to join her. The drumming was so loud that conversation was impossible. But every so often one of the young men or girls would come and urge me back into the dance.

We proceeded very slowly up to the main road and along it. Every so often the drummers stopped and stood still, their drumming grew even more frantic, sweat streamed down their faces and bare arms, and more and more people joined the dancing. One of the smaller drummers gave up and handed his drum to another boy, who had been waiting patiently for his turn.

Several of the local men marshalled the procession, led by one who seemed to be in charge of the whole celebration. He was a handsome dark-haired man, probably in his fifties, and I christened him 'the Elder'. He stopped us at road junctions until it was safe to cross, and firmly ejected one man, who was not from our locality, who tried to join the dancing. The inner lane of the road seemed to be reserved for us, and I saw a police sign saying 'No entry: procession'. At a big crossroads the police were out in force, stopping the traffic so that we could turn right. We passed through an area where there were shops and restaurants, and people stopped to look, and came out of the restaurants to watch us go by.

I do not know how long we walked and danced, though it must have been for nearly two hours. I was unaware of tiredness, and lost all sense of time. The drumming was mesmerising, and I felt completely absorbed into this ritual. Eventually we turned off into a smaller road which led to the lake. The crowds were thicker than ever here, and a lorry carrying another group's Durga was in front of our procession. Our friends told us to stay close to them so that we would not get lost.

At the lakeside I was encouraged to move right to the front, so that I could see what was happening. The lorry backed up to the *ghat*, and I was warned not to stand on the steps at the edge of the water because they were very slippery. The dark expanse of the lake stretched before me, carrying a flotsam of coloured rags and tinsel – the detritus of Durgas already immersed.

When Durga was hauled out of the lorry the Elder stood before her, blessed himself, said a prayer and touched his forehead to each of her shoulders in turn. Then she was pulled down the steps, turned round three times, splashed backwards into the water, and pushed out with long bamboo poles. Her sons followed, with less ceremony.

Now it was over, and the Elder introduced me to one of the women and told me to stay very close to her. She led me through throngs of people to where our lorries were now parked, and I was helped up into the back of one of them. I stood with Johanna, hanging onto the sides, as the lorry made its bumpy way home. Everyone was excited and talkative. Those next to us wanted to know what we had thought of the ceremony.

"Did you enjoy it?" they asked, and others thanked us for participating in their festival.

Back at the *pandal* the Elder said:

"Don't go yet. There is a final piece of the ceremony. You must wait because we are going to have a sweet distributed."

After a few minutes a woman came and sat in front of the *pandal* with a big bowl, and I queued up with the others, to have a sticky *gulab jamun* placed in my open hand. After that it really was the end of the ceremony, and we hurried home to wash the syrup off our hands and fall into bed.

* * *

The following day was a Sunday, and Johanna, Tracy and I decided to eat out in the evening. Tracy did not like Indian food, so we took a taxi to an Italian restaurant not too far away. (I had never had stomach problems in India before, but I was uncomfortable several times in Kolkata. The strange mixture of Indian and European food I was eating did not agree with me.)

We left the restaurant just before half past nine, and the girls wanted to buy a bottle of wine, so we looked for one of the licensed liquor stores. The wooden steps leading up to a building with two open hatches were crowded with young men, who looked at us curiously. They were buying whiskey. One of the salesmen saw us as we neared the top of the steps, beckoned us forward, hastily produced the desired bottle of wine, and sent us away. I got the impression that women were not expected to frequent liquor stores.

Now we needed a taxi, but any we saw were either already taken or drove straight past us. A young Indian couple was also trying to hail a taxi.

"It is very difficult to get one after nine thirty in the evening," the girl told us.

We decided we would have to walk home – it would not take more than half an hour. But we came to a crossroads where we would have to turn down a dark, ill-lit road between two ponds. It was completely empty of traffic and pedestrians. We could not see the far end where it joined the big busy road near our apartment, and the two girls were very apprehensive. There was a police checkpoint in a small building, and we decided it would be better to wait there until we could get a taxi.

A man, busy on his mobile phone, asked us where we were going, and a few minutes later a big car drew up, and he offered us a lift. However, we all felt it unwise to get into a car with a complete stranger. He was trying to persuade us when salvation appeared, in the person of the Elder from the day before. He was on his moped and stopped to see what was going on. When he understood, he said:

"I will escort you."

The other car drove away, and the Elder drove slowly ahead of us, stopping every now and again so that we could catch up.

"I can't drive beside you," he said. "People would think I was following you."

When we reached the brightly lit and crowded road near home he left us. We thanked him profusely, but he said:

"I know you, and I know you are good people and our guests. I couldn't leave you to walk by yourselves along that dark empty street."

It was comforting to feel that we belonged to the local community and that they were interested in our welfare.

* * *

A couple of days after the immersion ceremony I was introduced to Ravi, an eleven-year-old boy in one of Hope's boys' homes. He had muscular dystrophy, which was now affecting his legs so that he was unable to walk. Members of staff or other boys would lift him up and carry him from place to place. His father had brought him to the home because, living on the street, he could no longer look after an incurably sick child. His mother had died. But Ravi, though quiet, was bright and cheerful. He had been receiving tuition from volunteers while the other boys in the home went out to school, and I was to take over his lessons.

I was shown into a bright room, where there were three bunk beds with colourful bed covers. Ravi was sitting on one of the lower bunks, and he showed me his books and other possessions which he kept in a big drawer under the bed. He had workbooks for Maths and English, and was clearly well up to standard in these subjects. Though his spoken English was limited, his understanding of the language was much better than that of the children I had taught in the villages, and his reading and spelling were good. He could write in English and Bengali, and also speak some Hindi, though he did not write it. (It had been a shock to me when I arrived in Kolkata to discover that the Bengali script was different from the Devanagari in which Hindi is written, so that I was unable to read street signs and notices.)

Over the next few weeks I visited Ravi every weekday morning. He had recently spent some time in hospital, and tired easily, so I limited my teaching to little more than an hour a day. Schools were closed for much of the month of October, as the time between *Durgapuja*, at the start of the month, and *Kalipuja*, near the end, was a holiday period, similar to our week between Christmas and New Year, but lasting longer. So the other boys in the home were not at school, and Ravi, understandably, did not want to do school lessons. But he was keen to write letters to past volunteers who had taught him, so I bought writing paper and envelopes. He knew what he wanted to say, but he wanted me to help.

"Dear Susan Aunty," he wrote in neat writing, saying each word as he wrote it. "How are you? I am Fine. I Liked your Letter. When you Come in March Please Bring me a Birthday Gift."

My fears were confirmed – when I had looked at his exercise book, the English words in the lists he had written there all started with a capital letter. I decided that now, while he was busy composing his letter, was not a good time to explain when capitals were needed and when they were not.

Over three days he painstakingly wrote three letters to past volunteers, which were eventually delivered through Hope's office in Ireland.

The stories in his English workbook were rather boring and trivial, so I looked for more stimulating books to read with him. I found an illustrated encyclopedia in the home's library, and he was fascinated by the sections on dinosaurs, mountains and volcanoes, rivers and oceans, and on the human body. So at the weekend I visited the Oxford Book Company in the centre of the city and found books on wonders of the world, electricity, the planets, space flight, and so on.

Other boys would gather round to see what we were reading, and as I explained things to him in English Ravi would translate into Bengali for their benefit. He was an intelligent child and took a great interest in finding out more about the world around him.

The other boys in the home knew me as 'Ravi Aunty', and Johanna, who taught some of the children violin in the same home, was known as 'Violin Aunty'. They always put 'Aunty' or 'Uncle' second, after the identifying name. They are honorifics in India and, to be polite, children will address even adults they do not know as Aunty or Uncle.

While it was sad to see Ravi ill and unable to live a normal and active life, the situation of some of the boys in another home was heartbreaking. These children had been rescued from terrible and traumatic situations.

In a room on the first floor I met half a dozen young boys with a variety of psychological problems. Two were orphans who had been abandoned on the street, others came from abusive homes, and one had a severe hearing impairment and marks on his face that look like scars from old burns. A house mother sat in a corner where there was a television. The boys all jumped up from their play with cries of "Aunty, Aunty" as I appeared. They could not communicate very well, but they always called out in greeting to any volunteer who visited them.

One day I met a woman who was their counsellor and asked her what they were like when she first met them.

"They were all traumatised and very withdrawn," she said. "One of them just cried solidly for the whole of the first two weeks. He did not speak and was incontinent and self-harming – he had dark bite marks on his arms."

"What do you do in such a case?" I asked.

"I just sat beside him very quietly every day, until at last he began to relax," she replied. "Now he no longer wets his bed, and he does not often bite himself. But he does not speak much."

I was impressed by the changes brought about in these boys who had suffered so much in ways I could not begin to imagine. They always smiled when I visited and wanted me to join in their play. They had building blocks and a train set, and crayons to colour with. Their games were more appropriate to three- or four-year-olds than children aged seven or more. But at least, here in the home, they now had a chance to play and feel safe.

Upstairs there were teenage boys, some of whom had been living by the railway and had suffered dreadful injuries resulting in amputation of a leg or an arm, or in one case both an arm and a leg. Railway children risk being hit by trains or falling from them, and become addicted to sniffing solvents which can lead to harder drugs. These boys had graduated from Hope's drug rehabilitation centre and were now at school.

One attractive boy, with one leg amputated above the knee, shook my hand and greeted me first in Hindi and then English, telling me his name and asking mine. But when I complimented him on being able to speak three languages he replied, in English:

"No, I really only speak two – Hindi and Bengali."

Two little girls, around eight or nine years old, lay in cots in the small women's ward of the Hope hospital. One had been treated for Hodgkin's lymphoma, and her hair was only just beginning to grow again. She smiled when I arrived, and sat up to show me her treasures in a plastic bag at the end of her bed – red nail varnish, earrings, bangles and *bindis*. But she had little energy and soon lay down again. The other child was a bright and cheerful little thing, but she had been born with one leg very much shorter than the other, and doctors were performing a long series of operations so that she would be able to walk properly.

The ceiling of the ward was being painted, and nurses covered one end of the cots with plastic sheeting to protect them from the drips. The little girls thought this very funny, and laughed even more when their cots were moved to the other side of the ward as the painting progressed. A woman in a cotton sari followed the painter round with a cloth, wiping up any drops that fell on the floor.

On the floor above was the men's ward and a very small boy who had been found deserted in the street some months before. He suffered from cerebral palsy, could not speak and would never be able to walk, but he smiled and clapped his hands when anyone talked to him. This child had been cared for by the dedicated hospital staff since he was found.

The hospital only had sixteen beds in each of the two wards, and four high-dependency beds on the top floor next to the modern, well equipped operating theatre. The standard of care was extremely good, and the CEO told us that they could perform almost any type of operation, including spinal and brain surgery, but not cardiac operations.

"We have had no case of hospital-acquired sepsis since we opened eight years ago," he announced proudly.

This amazed a visiting nurse from one of the big Dublin hospitals.

"We have cases every week where I work," she said.

The whole hospital was clean and bright – a complete contrast to the dusty grey concrete hospital which I had attended in Palampur when I injured my ankle. Local people flocked to the outpatients and pharmacy on the ground floor. Those who could afford it paid for the services and medicines, which helped with the running costs.

* * *

On one occasion I was taken to visit a slum, though I never taught there. The street people lived beneath bridges, or in open spaces beside the road, with a covering of heavy plastic sheeting. It was not a very good protection from the monsoon rains. The slum, however, consisted of small cubical concrete houses, which provided more shelter.

I was taken into one building which was being used as a school. At one end sat five small children, with an Indian lady who was teaching them the English alphabet. They and their clothes were clean, in spite of the squalor they lived in. One boy was very shy, and hid his face when I asked him to tell me what he was learning, but a little girl piped up with, "A for apple, B for ball."

At the other end of the room several teenage girls were learning to read and write in Hindi. Their own language would have been Bengali, written in its own script. It was encouraging to see that girls in this slum were being given the chance to acquire an education.

The slum was beside a canal. Some charitable organisation had built a public sanitation block for them, but the effluent all emptied into the canal. The local chief minister, a woman, wanted to 'beautify' the area and build a promenade beside the canal. This meant that the inhabitants were in danger of being evicted. Their tiny houses would be razed to the ground, but there was no suggestion that alternative accommodation would be offered to them. These low caste people have no rights or protection.

* * *

Although the monsoon should have been over by the time I arrived, the rains were lingering late that year. The temperature was above thirty degrees centigrade, humidity was over ninety per cent, and almost every day there was a shower that lasted an hour or so. One day the downpour was so torrential that I was able to catch the teeming rain on camera. Huge brown dragonflies flew here and there beyond the balcony in the moist atmosphere. We needed the fans on in the apartment whenever we were home. Although there were air conditioners in the bedrooms, I found it more comfortable to sleep with the fan on, and only occasionally used the air conditioner to cool the room down before going to bed. I was sticky all the time, but coped with the humidity better than I had expected. The weather did not become cooler or less humid until I had been there three weeks.

There are trees everywhere in Kolkata, mynahs strutting and squabbling like starlings, and after dark the chirring of cicadas. From the balcony of the apartment I looked across at the fresh green of a tree on the opposite side of the lane, and the bare trunk of a palm beside it. Two mynahs came to roost on the leafy branches every day, sidling up to one another and rubbing their heads together in an affectionate way. Occasionally I would catch a glimpse of a tiny yellow-green bird hiding among the leaves, and once I saw a red-vented bulbul. A rather scruffy black kite often perched on the black plastic water tank on the roof opposite. But the most unlikely visitor was a small woodpecker which came one day to search for insects on the trunk of the palm tree.

I found Kolkata a strange city. There is no ancient Indian fort or maharaja's palace, for the East India Company created Calcutta in the eighteenth century from three little villages beside the Hooghly river, and it became the capital of British India until Delhi replaced it in 1911. So the architecture of all the big buildings is British. The fort in the huge grassy space of the Maidan, on the banks of the river, was built by the British on the site of the original East India Company's mud fort. It now houses the Eastern Command of the Indian Army. There is a polo ground and a racecourse, and at the northern end of the Maidan is a huge cricket stadium where international matches are played.

The East India Company's clerks lived and worked in the massive Writers' Building in the city centre. This, like the nineteenth century High Court, is a red brick building with ornate cream trimmings, vaguely reminiscent of the rippled brick effect on Keble College Oxford. The General Post Office and the Victoria Memorial, built of white marble, have great domes and neo-classical pillars. St John's Church is the oldest Anglican parish church in India, with memorial plaques on its walls dating back to the eighteenth century, and one, entirely in Latin, carrying the date 1697. Another records the death of a seven-month-old child 'from the sheer want of proper nutriment', and also her mother, 'during the sad and disastrous siege of Lucknow'. The obelisk in memory of those who perished in the Black Hole of Calcutta is now in the church grounds, though it was originally situated near the site of the Black Hole, close to the GPO.

Bright modern shops and shopping malls co-exist with small dark establishments selling food, cheap clothes and household goods, or providing photocopying or mobile phone services. A large shopping mall a short *tuk-tuk* ride from where I lived had a Marks and Spencer store, and European as well as Indian products in the food and grocery section. It was clean and bright and not unlike a mall at home, except for the security check at the entrance. I had to pass through an airport-style metal-detecting arch, and my bag was inspected – not unusual at entrances to public buildings in India, as they are on constant alert for terrorists. But I suspect these checks also ensured that only those who looked prosperous enough to buy things inside were admitted. When I bought books for Ravi, or cereal for breakfast, my purchases would be placed in a bag and I would have to display my receipt to the security guard at the shop door, who would then clip the bag closed. Nobody could get out of a store without proving they had paid.

There were smart clothes shops, several opticians and another mall along a main road near the Hope café. But in the afternoons the roadside became a fruit and vegetable market. I would see men setting shallow baskets on the ground at the edge of the road. They lined them with banana leaves, which they sprayed with water, before filling them with tomatoes, aubergines of different shapes and sizes, all sorts of gourds, cabbages, cauliflowers and potatoes. This was the best place to buy fresh vegetables, and if I asked how to cook an unfamiliar gourd one of the other customers was sure to stop and explain to me exactly how it should be treated. Small gourds, like tiny cucumbers with a starry cross-section, were to be sliced thinly and fried in butter. They had a slightly bitter taste. Other bigger gourds turned out to have the consistency of courgettes and were a delicious addition to a vegetable curry.

Further up this road the shops were replaced by a covered market. Stalls on either side of the pavement sold tunics and trousers, *salwar kameez* and saris, cheap jewellery, books, plastic buckets and boxes, china and glass. It was fascinating to push my way through the colourful crowd of busy shoppers, with all view of the road hidden behind the canvas walls of the stalls, and the sky obscured by heavy plastic roofing.

Travelling on the metro was a revelation. From the heat and dirt of the street I walked down steps into a cool, clean, shiny station, with paved floors and tiled walls. The name of the station was given on the walls in Hindi and English, as well as Bengali, and I began to make sense of the Bengali script by comparing it to the Hindi. Notices prohibited photography and spitting. At the Kalighat station there was an airport-style X-ray machine, through which some travellers sent their bags. It seemed a rather haphazard security system, as others simply walked past it with what they were carrying.

The machines where I placed my travel card were very quick and efficient. The gate would open immediately, and close ready for the next person the minute I was through. The machines in Dublin Dart stations seem sluggish in comparison. The trains were very frequent too. I usually waited no more than a couple of minutes for one to arrive, and on a Sunday, when there were far fewer travellers, the interval between trains was six minutes.

The trains were long and packed to bursting. Every carriage had a 'Ladies only' section, though as I usually got off at the second stop I did not move into it. Instead I stood as close to the door as possible, to make sure I would be able to get off the train.

I found other passengers very helpful. On one occasion, when I travelled in to the centre of the city, I was not sure which side the platform would be on when I reached my destination. It varied from station to station, but not in any regular way that I could see. As we neared my stop I moved towards one side of the carriage, but a man standing nearby called to me:

"You must get off at the other side."

Running to board a train which was overflowing with people one day, I reached the carriage door as it started to close. But a young man standing just inside grabbed me by the shoulders and hauled me into the carriage.

One weekend I was taken on a fascinating tour of the city by a delightful woman. She was a historian and explained to me that the names of streets reflected the history of the city. Some still bore the English names they were given originally, while others had had their names changed to Indian ones after Independence. The years when West Bengal had a communist government transformed Harrington Street to Ho Chi Minh Sarani, and Dharmatala Street to Lenin Sarani. But now the communists had been voted out (in the same way as they came to power – in a democratic election) and the new government was planning to remove the names they had imposed.

She took me to the busy wholesale flower market, where we wandered along lanes between tarpaulin-covered areas where men sat surrounded by open sacks of flowers. Some were piled with scarlet blossoms, others with yellow, and yet others with green leaves. A man passed me with marigold garlands slung over his shoulder. At one stall unopened lotus blossoms were piled on huge lily leaves, and at another two men sat cross-legged on the ground weighing out a mixture of red, white and magenta flowers in hand-held scales. They poured flower heads into one basket until they balanced a weight in the other.

Then we visited a place north of the city centre where the effigies of gods, animals and men were made for feasts such as *Durgapuja* or weddings. Here I saw piles of muddy clay, dredged from the river, waiting to be used to coat straw figures on bamboo frames. Layer after layer of mud is plastered on to build up the figure, finally producing a china-smooth finish which, when it has dried, is painted in bright colours. Beside the street and inside open workshops I saw goddesses and gods, lions and elephants, all in various stages of creation. Disembodied heads, hands and feet stood drying, waiting to be attached to the body of a goddess before she was painted and clothed. In an open-fronted room men were making the final glittering decorations and accessories for the statues.

* * *

Because of the holidays it was not until my third week in Kolkata that I started teaching in the coaching centres. These *nabadishas* are supported by the local police, who provide a room where street children can come for help from teachers and volunteers. Fewer children than usual attended during the time I was there, because of the school holidays. But I was able to help some young children with their maths, and older ones with their English.

I was told that one five-year-old girl was very slow at maths. She enjoyed counting out the little plastic cubes I brought along, and was able to count up to twelve in English.

"Pick up two cubes," I said. Then I gave her four more. "How many have you got now?"

"One, two, three, four, five, SIX!" she shouted proudly.

But if I asked her to write a six, she could not do it. Nor could she recognise a figure six unless she counted up to it in the sequence of figures 1, 2, 3, 4, 5, 6. I eventually discovered that in Bengal the children are taught maths using Bengali numbers, rather than our Arabic ones, until they are in fourth class. The children in Rajasthan and Himachal Pradesh were taught using Arabic numbers (which are actually based on ancient Indian ones) so they did not have the difficulty of doing maths with two different systems of figures. Bengali numbers are particularly confusing, since their figure four looks like our 8, and their seven is similar to our 9. English is taught as soon as the children start school, and unfortunately they are taught our numbers as well as our alphabet. So they not only have the difficulty of two alphabets, but also of two number systems. It did not surprise me that some of the children were having difficulty with their maths.

Some fifteen-year-olds were preparing for an important public examination, similar to our Junior Certificate, and came for help with their revision. The English syllabus for this exam seemed to owe a lot to British colonial ideas of education. The teenagers I helped were studying Kipling's poem *If*, Wordsworth's *Daffodils* and Oscar Wilde's *The Selfish Giant*.

I was impressed by their standard of English. They all spoke Bengali of course, but several spoke Hindi at home, as their families originated from the Delhi area. These children were attending a private school where teaching was through Hindi. The Government schools in West Bengal all teach through Bengali. But Hope provides sponsors to meet the cost of private education for those children who would benefit from it.

One afternoon, while I helped teenagers with their English, a very small girl arrived at the *nabadisha* wearing a pretty dress and with a ribbon in her dark hair. She started to read to the teacher in English from a book of nursery rhymes, showing off her accomplishment and performing for her audience. My teenage boys were very amused by her. The teacher explained to me:

"She is five and goes to an English medium school."

"Isn't that very expensive?" I asked.

"Yes, but she is very clever, and Hope has found her a sponsor. It is no use starting children in an English school later than five or six. It would be too hard for them to catch up, since their parents do not speak English and may even be completely illiterate."

It was hard to remember that these children lived on the street. They were always clean and tidily dressed, very polite and pleasant to talk to, and they were keen to get an education. When I asked two lads working for their school leaving exam what they were going to do next, they explained that they wanted to go on to study computing.

These children had perseverance and an ambition to make a better life for themselves. Others drop out of education, in spite of the help and encouragement offered by Hope. One evening I was with Maureen, Hope's founder, when we met a teenage boy that she knew. He had dropped out of school after second class and was selling incense sticks outside the restaurant where we had been eating. He spoke little English, but Maureen discovered that he lived with his family under the big road bridge nearby, where his father sold fish.

"He started school late and was much older than the others in his class," Maureen told me. "His parents don't understand the importance of education."

She urged the boy to go to the local *nabadisha* next day, where they would try to find him some way to continue his education with others closer to his own age. But he did not turn up.

One afternoon at the *nabadisha* a group of four fifteen-year-olds, three boys and one girl, engaged me in conversation to practise their English. One of the boys started the discussion:

"Indian culture is bad," he said.

"It can't be all bad," I replied.

"Well, what is good about it?"

"Close family ties and support?" I suggested. (I knew that the group I was talking to all lived with their parents and siblings on the street.)

The others nodded in agreement, and one said:

"Yes, our families and our friends on the street – we all look out for one another."

But not all street children have loving and supportive families. I heard of one fourteen-year-old girl who had been taken into the care of one of the girls' homes. She was allowed to leave the home to spend some of the holiday with her mother, on the strict understanding that her psychotic and violent father would not be allowed near her. But she returned to the home traumatised – her mother had 'married' her to a man of her acquaintance over the weekend.

* * *

Strings of yellow lights made a ceiling for the laneway near my apartment, rows of little candles glimmered on every balcony, coloured lights blazed on distant apartment blocks, and fireworks burst in cascades of red, blue, green and yellow in the dark sky overhead. It was the evening of Divali, the Festival of Lights. Johanna, Samantha and I took the little boys from the nearby Hope home to see the sights, accompanied by one of the 'uncles' who cared for them.

Everyone was out on the streets. People were placing little pyramids on the roadway and lighting them, then standing back as, with a loud bang, a golden fountain burst out, sometimes reaching twice the height of a man. The little boys loved it. They smiled and clapped their hands at every firework. All of them except the deaf boy. He seemed rather withdrawn that evening, and he backed away warily whenever one of the street fireworks was lit, even though we stood well out of range. I tried to stay by him, and encouraged him back to the others when the golden sparks died away.

In Kolkata, Divali is almost eclipsed by *Kalipuja*, which always coincides with it. No sooner had our local Durga *pandal* been taken down than men had started to erect one for Kali. New holes were dug for a new set of bamboo poles, and the structure was walled with expanded polystyrene, coated with smooth plaster and painted in black with scarlet decorations. For Kali is a black goddess, her hands stained red with blood, wearing a belt of human skulls, and with her red tongue sticking out in surprise as she stands on the body of Shiva, her husband, who has lain down before her to stop her killing spree. She is the dark incarnation of

Durga, and empowers her devotees, taking away their fear of time and death. *Kalipuja*, like *Durgapuja*, is a festival that lasts several days and culminates with the immersion of the goddess.

Kalighat, south of the city centre, was an ancient site of pilgrimage on the banks of the Hooghly long before the East India Company arrived. Now the river has retreated to the west, but there is still a temple to Kali there. I barely glimpsed the dark statue of the goddess through the thronging crowds of pilgrims. She no longer receives human sacrifices, but as I walked back to where I had left my shoes I came upon a small black goat with scarlet hibiscus flowers strewn over its back. Its owner looked on as a priest squatted at its head, caressing it and praying, preparing it for sacrifice. Behind him two U-shaped pieces of wood were stained rusty brown, one with a small U where the little goat would be decapitated with one blow, and the other for larger sacrificial animals. A goat is sacrificed in this temple every day and the meat distributed to devotees.

Gora, the Indian staff member who lived at the other end of our apartment, invited us all to his family home for the final evening of *Kalipuja* and the immersion – in the river this time. The Hooghly is a western branch of the Ganges as it enters the delta, where the Brahmaputra joins it to flow into the Bay of Bengal. So, as far as the immersion ceremony is concerned, the river flowing through Kolkata is the holy Ganga.

A large *pandal* had been erected outside the family home, extending out across the pavement. As we arrived two *Baul* singers were performing, dressed in orange robes, one of them playing an instrument something like a lute. The songs belong to an oral folk tradition, associated with mystic teaching.

The music was very loud, and after greeting Gora's mother I went upstairs to a room where a man and woman were performing, the man playing a ukelele and the woman an Irish harp. She explained that she was half Indian and half Irish. They were playing and singing American and European songs. Up another flight of stairs the flat roof had been covered over, and we ate a feast of vegetarian food within a marquee. Here we could drink the water they brought, for the house had a purifier in the kitchen.

Later I went down to the *pandal* where Kali was being prepared for her departure, wreathed in incense. Big brown butterflies flitted around, trying to find a way out into fresh air. There was drumming and music, and people danced and waved lamps in front of the goddess. Finally, several strong men lifted her and carried her outside to where her lorry waited under skeins of green lights.

I joined the drummers and the people dancing behind them. As we went, one man or another would light one of the golden fountains I had seen on Divali and kick its embers into the side of the road when it was over. This time we only processed round the block, as the river was too far away to walk there. Then I was helped up into the back of the lorry carrying Kali. Several men lay at her feet resting and sleeping. They had been hired from outside the city as bearers for the heavy effigy.

Beside the river a group of white-uniformed police watched over the proceedings. The river was dark and wide, with lights sparkling in the distance on the far bank. The bearers woke up and heaved Kali down the steps to the riverbank, to the sound of drumming and ululation. With some difficulty, for she was very heavy, she was rotated three times. Then a rope was passed behind her shoulders so that she could be lowered into the water. As she splashed in, men who had been filling bottles from the holy Ganga sprayed the watching crowd. A boat pulled out to push Kali into the main current, and the immersion was over. I was told that the effigy would be fished out of the river further down and disposed of in a more ecological manner.

* * *

Samantha decided to celebrate Hallowe'en Irish style. She managed to find a beautiful big pumpkin and took it to show the boys in the Hope home round the corner.

"Can I have it to cook for the boys' dinner?" pleaded the cook when he saw it.

"No, it's not for eating."

"Not for eating? What is it for, then?"

Everyone watched as she carved a face in it and hollowed it out to place a candle inside. When it was lit, and the face illuminated by the flickering flame, the little boys clapped their hands. But to the cook it must have seemed incomprehensible that good food should be wasted in this way, though he managed to collect the pieces hollowed out from inside.

* * *

The end of the month also saw Hope's annual celebration of its foundation. Children from the street and the boys' and girls' homes had been practising their dances for weeks, which had further depleted the holiday-time attendance at the *nabadishas*.

On the day itself visitors and volunteers were treated to a cruise on the river. We embarked on a smart white cruiser at a *ghat* between the two bridges – the Howrah bridge and the modern one further downstream, inaugurated in 1992. In Kolkata the Hooghly is so wide that there was no bridge until 1874, when a pontoon bridge was constructed to connect the city to the big Howrah railway station on the west bank. This was replaced in 1943 by the Howrah bridge – at that time the longest cantilever bridge in the world. But as we steamed upstream we crossed the paths of several rather dilapidated ferries, still carrying crowds of people across the river.

I stood at the rail and watched as little green islands of leafy branches floated by on the swirling brown current, and a lovely old sailing boat, with a red, green and pink striped sail, flew downstream. Two men were fishing from a tiny rowing boat, while behind them a refuse tip covered the steep bank from the road down to the water's edge. Further out from the bank a group of derelict rusting hulks was waiting to be demolished and their metal recycled. Far away on the opposite bank rose the red brick bulk of the Howrah railway station, and as we passed under the Howrah bridge I looked up at the never-ending traffic of cars, buses and mopeds, and the pedestrians streaming across on the footpath, some carrying huge loads on their heads.

On the near bank we passed a temple, and then the burning *ghat* where the bodies of the wealthy are cremated on wooden pyres. Here, unlike at Varanasi, the pyres are hidden by a wall, and all I could see was smoke rising into the air from two fires. Wood is expensive, and those who are not well-off are consigned at the nearby electric crematorium. But the ashes of all can be scattered on the Ganges/Hooghly.

That evening, dressed in beautiful saris, Johanna, Samantha and I set off for the Foundation Day celebrations. The kindly woman who kept a tiny shop close to our apartment had helped us to dress. She had ushered us into the room behind her shop where she and her husband lived. It was almost filled with a double bed, but there were cupboards on the walls, and a full-length mirror where we could admire our reflections once we were dressed. Putting on a sari is not at all easy for the uninitiated, as there is an art to making and arranging the pleats at the front, and pins are needed to hold it at the shoulder. My sari was a deep turquoise, Johanna's was pine green, and Samantha's magenta, and all had gold trimmings.

As we entered the huge auditorium where the celebrations were being held, the little boys from the local home waved to us excitedly, and they all had to be hugged before we were ushered to front row seats. First there were speeches – mercifully short and to the point – and then a magnificent display of songs and traditional dances.

I was amazed at how expertly these children coordinated intricate movements of their hands, bodies and feet. They were dressed in magnificent costumes and put their hearts into the performance.

* * *

Though I enjoyed the experience of working for Hope, I felt that I had not done as much for the children in Kolkata as I had in the village schools. This was partly because I was there for only five weeks, much of which was holiday time. Ravi was the only child I had worked with regularly during my stay. The attendance at the *nabadishas* varied because of the holidays, and I never worked with the same children for more than two or three sessions. Many of them I only met once.

But Hope has a permanent Indian staff on the ground, which provides the continuity essential for the success of the charity's work. The volunteer organisation with which I worked in Rajasthan and Himachal Pradesh could not offer such continuous and permanent help to the village schools and daycare centres. When there was not a sufficient number of volunteers, some schools lost their help with English teaching. The number of volunteers varies from year to year and month to month, and the numbers choosing to work in India are small in comparison with those going to Vietnam, or African and South American countries. As far as I know, the camp at Shiv was never reopened after the damage caused by the 2010 monsoon, and the camp near Lalsot has since been closed as well.

On this occasion I worked in a big city for the first time and met children who lived on the street and in Hope's homes. The contrast with the rural villages where I had taught in other years was enormous. But once more I encountered polite, friendly children, all eager to learn. An Australian visitor, who happened to wander into the Hope café while she was in Kolkata, chatted with some of the volunteers.

"Why do you try to teach these children?" she asked. "They are only street children. They won't have the intelligence to benefit from a proper education."

She horrified all of us, and she could not have been more wrong. There was the same range of intelligence among the children I taught, in Kolkata as well as in the villages, as in any similar group of children in Ireland. The main difference I found was the Indian children's enjoyment of school and keen attention in lessons.

As always, I was sad to leave India. But there was a magic moment as I gazed out of the window on my flight back to Delhi. There, towering above a bank of cloud, brilliantly white against a blue sky, were the snow-clad peaks of the high Himalaya. First the long mass of Kanchenjunga, and then, unmistakably, Everest.

"I will come back," I promised myself.

EPILOGUE

Western visitors to India seem to fall into two distinct groups: those who love the country, and those who hate it.

"I will never go back to India. I cannot bear the sight of so much misery," an Irish friend told me.

Others cite, as the reason for their aversion to the country, the endemic corruption, the violence and discrimination against women and those of lower caste, the dirt and the desperate poverty.

However, we in Ireland are not exempt from corruption and sexual abuse, though nobody would accuse the majority of the Irish population of such behaviour. What might an Indian think of Ireland if all he knew of it was what was reported in our newspapers – rapes, murders, the abuse of children by the Church and of the elderly and disabled in state institutions?

There is poverty here, too, and families made homeless. Discrimination against Travellers is discrimination on the basis of caste. We may exclaim in horror, but we recognise that there is good as well as bad in our society. So many of us have friends and families and lead safe, comfortable lives. It is only too easy to become inured to the injustice in our own culture, to turn a blind eye to beggars on the street, or to think that the government must do something about homelessness, while objecting to the provision of emergency housing in our own area.

The problems in India are on a much larger scale, as is the population (well over a billion). Corruption is rife and permeates all levels of society. The enormous gulf between rich and poor is increasing unrelentingly. Although my middle-class neighbours in Kolkata were not extremely wealthy, they could afford to buy computers and cars, and fly between cities. For these things they pay prices similar to those we pay in Europe. There are other Indians who are exceedingly rich, even by European standards. Some billionaire businessmen and politicians live lives of privilege and luxury, matching and sometimes even exceeding the lifestyles of maharajas in the past. In contrast, one person in every five lives on less than one dollar a day[9].

Many people in rural areas live a hand-to-mouth existence, depending on subsistence farming. According to the 2011 census, over two-thirds of the Indian population is rural[10]. That means that for every town or city dweller there are two people living in villages in the countryside. This is in spite of the continual migration of people from the countryside to the cities.

But though there is desperate poverty and inequality, India does not leave me with feelings of despair and hopelessness. I discovered that poverty does not inevitably mean destitution. The people in the villages where I worked were certainly extremely poor and needed great improvements to their standard of living, income and healthcare. But they were not all demoralised and miserable. Each family had its own tiny house, and there were strong family and community bonds. They were hospitable and friendly, celebrated festivals with enthusiasm and made the most of what they had. Their positive attitude to life was an inspiration to me.

In those tiny communities there were no extreme differences between one house and another, or between the lifestyles of the

---

9 *UN Millenium Development Goals report for India*, compiled from the 2011 census. See http://mospi.nic.in/Mospi_New/upload/mdg_26feb15.pdf.

10 http://censusindia.gov.in/2011-prov-results/paper2/data_files/india/Rural_Urban_2011.pdf.

inhabitants. Even in Shiv, where the more prosperous could afford a television, a motorbike, or a new house, there were no signs of abject poverty and no-one living on the street.

People did not spend their time hankering after inessential luxuries. Our style of advertising breeds discontent, making people feel that they cannot be happy without the latest products that are being promoted. I found it liberating to live in a rural community, without the pressures of advertising, where small shops, if there were any, stocked little more that the necessities of daily life. Of course, India is not exempt from the pressures and pleasures of consumerism. But it is only an option for the better-off sections of society.

In cities, where people without proper homes live surrounded by those so much more affluent than themselves, there is undoubtedly much misery as well as poverty. There are some who are outcast – sick, disabled and destitute, with no friends or family to care for them. But in Kolkata so many of the poor people I encountered scraped a living by selling goods and services, and were ready to smile cheerfully.

The energy and resilience of these street people always amazed and impressed me, and I was struck by the honesty of so many people I met. One day I bought fruit at a tiny street stall, and was walking away with the coins I had been given in change when the stallholder ran after me.

"You need more change," he called, waving a ten rupee note.

I had handed him a twenty rupee note in mistake for a ten rupee one (they are almost the same colour), but he did not take advantage of my mistake, even though an extra ten rupees would have meant far more to him than it did to me.

The street people may be materially impoverished, but they do not lose their self-reliance or independence. There is a spirit of community among them. As one of the teenagers I taught said:

"Our family and friends on the street – we all look out for one another."

Though they are not provided with adequate physical shelter or any state aid, street and slum dwellers are able to cook their own meals, wash their own clothes and find ways to earn a little money.

What a contrast to families made homeless in Dublin. Unlike Indian street people, Irish families are given a roof over their heads. But often they are placed in hotels, where they cannot cook for themselves or do their own laundry. They may be moved far away from the area where their children go to school and where the parents have a chance of finding work. They have little control over their daily lives. This must lead to feelings of despair and a lack of self-reliance and self-esteem. For asylum seekers in direct provision who are not able to work, the psychological effects must be even worse. Though their need for physical shelter may be met, these homeless families and asylum seekers are psychologically and emotionally impoverished. These people in Ireland have less control over their own day-to-day existence than many of the street people in India.

It has been suggested that social inequality reduces happiness more than poverty alone[11]. In the consumer society in developed countries, levels of happiness do not increase indefinitely with increasing wealth. 'Keeping up with the Joneses' reduces people's satisfaction with their lives. In the tiny villages where I worked there was little evidence of significant social inequality. Perhaps the people I met there were happier in general than people in cities, where the gulf between rich and poor was so evident.

At a meeting in Dublin, a representative of one of the big aid agencies said:

"Many volunteers come home and say that the people they have worked with are happy, in spite of being poor. They have not understood anything about the lives of the people. They have not seen their needs. These people are not happy."

---

11 *The Spirit Level: Why equality is better for everyone*, by Richard Wilkinson and Kate Pickett, Penguin Books 2010. See in particular chapters 1 and 15.

If happiness means being content with one's life, with no pressing needs and no desire to change it in any way, then clearly he was right. And there are certainly people in India who live in misery and destitution, abandoned by society. But, as I discovered, this is not an inevitable result of poverty. In spite of their needs, the people I worked with did not live in despair. They had a sense of community and got on with their lives, doing what they could to improve their situation. They were ready to enjoy small pleasures that came their way.

I realised that happiness does not depend on having everything you want, or even everything you need. It is a state of mind, the way you approach life.

"I bring up my children to appreciate what they have in life, even though it may be very little," a man in one small town told me.

This seems to me to be the attitude to life that keeps people smiling in spite of their poverty. This positive way of thinking was summed up for me by an Indian friend, who said:

"Remember, this day, like every other, is a 'Today Only offer'. Don't miss out on it."

* * *

There is surely no country on earth that is exempt from poverty and discrimination. Though undoubtedly there are evils in Indian society, I have also seen good, and I love the country and its people.

When I think of India I think of warmth and colour – the rainbow hues of the women's saris, magenta bougainvillea tumbling over a garden wall, the luminous white of heavy-scented gardenia flowers in the dusk, the flash of turquoise as an India roller takes flight, the metallic purple of tiny hummingbirds, the crimson sun setting in the desert, and the azure blue of the sky above glittering snow on mountain peaks.

I remember the taste of spices – cumin and coriander, ginger and cardamom. I relive the excitement and liveliness of noisy and chaotic cities and of crowded and colourful markets. I hear again the cheerful chatter at the village pump.

I think of the people I have met, their friendliness to an outsider like myself, their strong family ties, their resourcefulness, their cheerfulness even in the face of adversity.

"India is so full of life," I exclaimed at the end of my first visit, and, after all my travels and volunteering, my lasting impression is of the exciting, colourful, chaotic vitality of the country.